LIFE FORCE

DATE			

LIFE FORCE
The World of Jainism

By Michael Tobias

Asian Humanities Press
Berkeley, California

ASIAN HUMANITIES PRESS

Asian Humanities Press offers to the specialist and the general reader alike, the best in new translations of major works and significant original contributions, to enhance our understanding of Asian literature, religions, cultures and thought.

PHOTO CREDITS: *Cover, Navin Kumar Gallery, New York; title page and chapter eight, Namita Jain.*

87313696

Library of Congress Cataloging-in-Publication Data

Tobias, Michael.
     Life Force : the world of Jainism / by Michael Tobias.
        p.   cm.
     Includes bibliographical references.
     ISBN 0-89581-899-X
     1. Jainism. I. Title.
BL 1351.2.T63 1991
294.4--dc20   91-18902
                                    CIP

BL
135.2
T63
1991

Printed in the United States of America

SPECIAL ACKNOWLEDGEMENTS

I WOULD LIKE TO THANK MY DEAREST FRIEND, MUSE, AND WIFE, Jane Gray Morrison, for her support, humor, astounding intellect, and even greater heart—for her own indescribable breed of 'Janeism', in other words.

I am indebted to all of those hundreds of good friends in India—far too numerous to mention here—who so helped me several years ago during the making of my PBS film, *Ahimsa: Non-Violence*. Some of those wonderful people are cited in this work.

I thank Robert Radin, long time spiritual mentor, co-adventurer, and poet of generous dimensions, for his sensitive photographic contributions to this volume.

And I thank the astute Julie Castiglia for putting me in touch with the publisher.

Finally, I am most grateful to the great scholar, Professor Padmanabh S. Jaini, of the University of California at Berkeley, not only for consulting on the film *Ahimsa*, but for constantly easing me beyond my own incessant idealism, which is so easily prone to mere naivety, or misconception. He has done so with good humor, wisdom, and with all the understanding and modesty one could ever hope for in a friend. Professor Jaini was kind enough to read this book in manuscript form in order to help rectify any scholarly and interpretive problems.

CONTENTS

P R E F A C E

THIS IS AN UNABASHED WORK. It heeds no stubborn objectivism, because my own experiences of Jainism have affected me greatly. The affection is everything. My aim is that such affection become contagious, meaningful to the point of action.

My previous doubts regarding humanity's willingness or capacity to live respectfully on this fragile bit of turf we call Earth have been stilled as a result of my increasing familiarity with Jain doctrine, and my many Jain friends. Something happened, somewhere, sometime. In the accumulation of contacts and sensations; that sudden click, a quiet revelation purring at the rear of that dark canyon I know to be myself; conveying what I must have known to be true all along. For as Blaise Pascal reminds us, we only search for that which we have already discovered.

The following work sets out to examine just what it means, according to the Jains, to live harmoniously, and how it is possible to do so in a world of contradiction and pain.

These "personal meditations" in no way purport to be a definitive work, but merely one westerner's interpretation of certain limited aspects of a complex Asian religion. I have placed these perceptions within a context of other religions and philosophies of non-violence and ecology. Any good university research library will yield to the inquiring student hundreds of authoritative texts in several western languages on the fine points of Jainism (though the majority of ancient and medieval commentaries and treatises have not as yet been translated into English, this representing fertile ground for future scholarship).

I have relied upon—and list in the footnotes—those seminal works which have been translated, or written by Jain scholars in English, and which I have largely relied upon. I have attempted to juxtapose some of those elements which I consider most important to my notion of a *life force*—an ethical, aesthetic, biological, indeed, comprehensive miracle of being—however simplistic and incomplete the present synthesis. That *life force*, I shall argue, suggests a mental rampart of effective conscience inherent to the human animal; an ameliorative impulse that has within its realm the capability of stepping away from an otherwise dangerous and relentless evolution. We can enlist an alternative ideal which I know to be humanity's forceful compassion; its innate desire to nurture and cherish that which is all around us. We need not brandish the instruments of pain, nor unwittingly succumb to the widespread abuse which everywhere goes by the names of progress, or political expediency, or right intentions. The heart is the mirror image of the *life force*. From childhood, every human being knows of this implacable catalyst for good, for joy; for unselfishly sustaining that which the universe has mysteriously conspired to foster in the name of life, here on Earth.

In my own exposure to Jain culture, I have probed into this *life force*, and its urgent relevance to the world at large; a world dominated by one species that is rapidly sapping the earth's ecological vitality.

Jains themselves have grown up with these concepts which I, a westerner, have only more recently struggled to understand.

In tracking a philosophy of biological ethics and spiritual ecology, which I read into Jainism, I have not adhered to a strictly academic train of thought. It is my own train of thought, and whatever confusion or wide blunders may inadvertently surface have their own subjective strengths and weaknesses; are part of a humble effort to convey a sense of that reverence which Jainism has given to me; a reverence for life which this religion of India has so uniquely articulated.

Dublin, Ireland
Spring, 1991

CHAPTER ONE

Ethical Realism

LIKE AN INNER JAPANESE GARDEN, with its profusion of miniature worlds, subtle moss species, restrained exuberance, and perfect orchestration—botanical life enshrined by the impulses of art, that art conversely canonized by life—Jainism, too, emerges as a secret refuge for plants and animals, an artistic oasis. This delicate balance spanning hope and despair does not brashly declare itself, nor go in for theatrics. Jainism—India's, and possibly the world's oldest religion—is a quiet, overwhelmingly serious way of life, a cultural insistence on compassion, a sociology of aesthetics that has dramatically changed the world, and will continue to effect change. Radical change. But it is no exclusive arboretum for gazing, either.

Jainism is a momentous example to all of us that there can, and does exist a successful, ecologically responsible way of life which is abundantly non-violent in thought, action and deed. We might misread our history, go forward confusedly to perpetrate other follies, but we will do so knowing that there is a viable alternative.

Human civilization is scattered with pyres of skepticism, premeditated paradox, singular schizophrenia. Our brain has wobbled feverishly between clashing rocks, dualing instincts, incontinence and glory; goaded on by the misconception that man is a carnivore at heart. At any one time, according to war historians, approximately half of the human population is directly or indirectly engaged in war. But we mustn't forget that the other half is engaged in peaceful activities. It is too easy to subsume the pleasure and recall only the pain. The slightest affirmation is fraught with overwhelmingly contrary evidence. And each new outbreak of war adds additional kindling to the dark and mounting philosophies of aggression which have in the twentieth-century been upheld as the most primeval and enduring mode of survival known to human nature. Military conquest— such as the coalition's victory over Iraq, with a resulting human death toll of nearly one-hundred thousand, and many, many more plant and animal species—inflates the tired Hobbesian rhetoric of a species which prefers to count its warheads, aerial sorties and POW's, rather than its blessings.

Jainism has helped me to see through these habitual presumptions. For many millennia, Jain logic has worked out a more complete picture of human experience that encompasses our capacity for compassion and upholds the faith in gentleness over the more ubiquitous, Clausewitzian arguments in defense of combat. We succumb to the sluggishness of tyranny through apathy and neglect. Jainism is about discipline and observance. Its revelations, injunctions, and points of view are not merely confined to the dry, bald corridors of academia, though Jain commentators are prolix, their myriad manuscripts totalling in the thousands of analytical and poetic volumes. But beyond this passion for learning and analysis, Jains themselves have actively sustained a staggeringly pure complexion of beliefs to astonish even the most veteran cynics. It is an eminently practical philosophy, as Mahatma Gandhi himself brilliantly proved.

Jainism is not cloaked in the negation of life that is so characteristic, say, of ancient desert Christianity, or Buddhism. There is nothing fatalistic about its philosophy of history, though it is quick to seize upon the weaknesses in human nature. What distinguishes Jain theology and praxis from all other religions is its emphasis on the immediate repercussions of one's behavior. The pain or pleasure of the world hangs in the balance of our thoughts and actions. With such importance attached to our being, every feeling, thinking individual must find himself endowed with enormous responsibilities, marooned on a mirror. In the end, Jains recognize that those responsibilities are to oneself. You can not save the world, but you can cultivate your own garden, which the Jains know to be the soul. And there is the indelible twist: one soul is equal to all souls.

The earth is comprised of this many-wedded soul whose cumulative reason for being is what I'm calling—and has been called—*the life force.*

We have one thing to accomplish in this generation: not our pleasure, but the pleasure of the world. We will not sleep until every creature can sleep peacefully. We will not eat before all creatures partake of the same nourishment. We will not abide a single instance of cruelty. We can not vouchsafe the lunacy, under any name, or any guise, which hails the abuse of this earth and all her goodness; this life force within us; this frenzy to be born, and re-born; to live and to die; to love and to understand. Short of these freedoms, our life is nothing. Without extending that hand of freedom to every other organism, there is no solace, can be no moment's respite.

Jains were undoubtedly among the first people to focus upon this incantation, these basic rights, this animal and plant liberation; upon the multifaceted realm of what today we term environmentalism. They worked out the principles of hygiene, equality of the sexes. And they may have been the first to liken the science of biology to the urgings of spirituality, an invigorating conjunction not readily acknowledged outside of the Jain community until the early twentieth century, in the works of Henri Bergson. Mahavira, the twenty-fourth Jain spiritual leader, a contemporary of Buddha, had stated, "One who neglects or disregards the existence of earth, air, fire, water and vegetation disregards his own existence which is entwined with them.."[1] Such declarations were basic to three-thousand year old Jain canons, as will be seen.

Jain art has similarly been far in advance of its time, both in its sculpture and painting. At the temple edifices of Mount Abu and Palitana; or in the manuscript illuminations painted between the fourteen-and-sixteenth centuries in the desert towns of western India, the Jain aesthetic sensibility translates its so called spiritual biology into a haven for the senses.

Jain politics and jurisprudence meanwhile elevate the concept of self-restraint to what should be, and at times—under the tutelage of numerous Jain kings—*was* national policy. In keeping with such policy, the Jains have recognized non-injury to all creatures (a principle called *ahimsa)* as the fundamental law—not only of our being, but of all nature. Ahimsa, say the Jains, is our only possible joy, our true salvation. And this preamble is based upon the spectacular realization that we humans are equipped with a conscience; we can make intelligent and sensitive choices. The fact of a fickle evolution is no excuse for bad behavior. Evolution does not condemn us to anything. Our choices condemn us, say the Jains. And thus, amid the tumultuous seas of nature, we are like an island of choice; Robinson Crusoes of decisiveness. We can self-destruct, or carry on. But we will not live on as a species if we fail to co-exist harmoniously with all other creatures sharing this island with us.

Unbounded enthusiasm is too frequently subject to the laws of skepticism in human culture. A thousand Gandhis might not have stopped a Hitler; and they certainly weren't what stopped Saddam Hussein. Three thousand years of ahimsa did not impede the outbreaks of terrible violence occasioning the partition of India with Pakistan. Moreover, centuries of seemingly benign relations in Germany did not prevent many (or most) of the Germans themselves from turning on their Jewish neighbors at the first opportunity during the 1930's and 40's. The same can be said with respect to other endemic hatreds too universal to enumerate. Jean Paul Sartre stated that even if there were no Jews, there would still be anti-Semitism.

For every philosophy of peace, there has always appeared a seemingly more powerful Caligula, Hideyoshi, Joseph McCarthy,

Nero, or Rasputin. A King Ashurnasirpal II (883-859 B.C.) flayed his victims, and was said to have impaled seven hundred prisoners one day atop towers surrounding the city gates of the Assyrian Empire, with the same relish I would point out, of later Parisians in the 1730s who apparently mutilated alley cats and disembowelled dogs in massive numbers because it was the vogue. Educated Athenians used to sacrifice young boys and girls to the gods. The Aztecs similarly slaughtered some 20,000 estimated victims every year to their own gods, fifty-five each day. Scholars suggest that some four million Aztecs were burned, their hearts cut out, the girls tortured and sexually cannibalized, then tossed dismembered into wells or off cliffs. Plentiful historical monuments attest to the same blood-lust that has most recently prompted the Iraqis to execute thousands of Kuwaitis, and prior to that, Iranians and Kurds; The Palette of Narmer, the bas-relief of Eannatum of Lagash, the stele of Naram-sin, Trajan's column, and the platform of Chichen which is decorated with a frieze of human skulls. Similar Hindu friezes attesting to the bloodshed inherent to the oldest Vedic literary epics can be seen at the Ellora Caves. Our modern military cemeteries and monuments—like that at today's Hiroshima—convey the same haunting ethos of horror.

Arnold Toynbee chronicled history's rampages, with its wave after wave of vicious warrior barbarians. Today, our violence continues, not only in the guise of war, but in the form of unbelievable animal abuse and murder, all perpetrated beneath the sadistic veneers of useless biomedical science, product and military testing, and grievous appetites. Every day, upwards of one million innocent, precious creatures are tortured and re-tortured, before dying in agonizing pain. Billions—BILLIONS—of individuals (each of whom a child could name, could stroke and love, but which society prefers to call poultry and livestock and seafood) have been systematically tortured and killed so that their filets can be consumed, where such meat lingers odiously for something like nine days in a human intestine before being cast out.

"Let the advocate of animal food force himself to a decisive experiment on its fitness," wrote the poet Percy Shelley. "Tear a living lamb with his teeth and plunging his head into its vitals, slake his thirst with the steaming blood; when fresh from the deed of horror let him revert to the irresistible instincts of nature that would rise in judgement against it, and say, Nature formed me for such work as this. Then, and then only, would he be consistent."[2]

Hunters will argue that they care the most about nature. Bolstered by government policies which begin by calling animals "game," and by political action committees devoted to the gun, our laws favor wanton massacre and the desensitizing of children to the miracle of life. Indeed, in most countries, the child is taught to look at nature as something to be captured, brought down, consumed.

Bullfighter-types, like Jose Ortega y Gasset, have celebrated the hunt, on the grounds that a man is not a man unless he's out murdering defenseless organisms. "When one is hunting," wrote Gasset in his *Meditation on Hunting*, "the air has another, more exquisite feel as it glides over the skin or enters the lungs; the rocks acquire a more expressive physiognomy, and the vegetation becomes loaded with meaning. All this is due to the fact that the hunter, while he advances or waits crouching, feels tied through the earth to the animal he pursues." Such rapture defends its flawed thinking on the basis of zoological analogy; that other animals kill one another in the wild for food, and thus, human hunters can feel similarly guiltless—naturalistic—in doing so. We are entitled by such logic to have the same primitive instincts and blood on our claws as red ants and tarantula wasps, pythons and falcons.

Furthermore, there is allegedly natural custom forming our behavior. Thus John Locke commented in *Some Thoughts Concerning Education*, that children love to "torment" animals "with a seeming kind of Pleasure," a penchant repeated throughout adulthood. With nearly two-hundred-million public firearms in the United States alone, Locke certainly had a point. Jains reject the validity of such illustrations. There may be a gruesome perpetuity in nature that can do nothing to impede the grizzly bear's cruel destruction of a moose. But there is no excuse for similar human behavior. We need to work out our own masterplan, say the Jains; ethical mandates which transcend the hardship and agony of nature. As a species capable of profound introspection, we should have outgrown the carnivore mentality. If we do not, then we will merely continue through the ages to wallow in our own blood. Or we will die out altogether. Some would say the sooner the better.

The ethological record of peaceful animal communions furthers the suspicion that even nature's masterplan is not so uniformly aggressive. While all organisms display a quality of irritability, more animals forage for their food than kill for it; symbiotic, and herbivorous animal and plant communities are more far-ranging than carnivorous ones. Ninety-eight percent of all energy transfer on earth—i.e., nutrition, survival—is the result of sunlight, water, carbon dioxide, and soil, not aggression. The overwhelming *weight* of the life force on earth is accounted for in peace-loving plants, not malevolent animals.[3]

According to Jainism, animals will eventually be re-born as human animals, at which time they will have to chose: empathy, peace, compassion—ahimsa—or perpetual degrees of violence. Humanity is the launching site for this choice. We have it in our power to reverse an evolutionary masterplan that is brutal, that needs fixing. The Jains have modelled themselves after a vision of nature that favors peace and love over war and hatred, and they have envisioned—indeed, realized—a major world religion whose guiding tenet is this heartfelt aspiration. The reader is likely to stop here and declare, 'But all religions—or certainly most of them—are about love. What's the big deal?' Jainism departs from this theoretical norm in one striking, and all-important manner: it has never deviated from its original pledge. If we can understand how an ancient, seemingly uncomplicated ethical position can continue to flourish in a more complex modernity, we will have accomplished a critical hurdle.

For the Jains, there would be no talk of altering nature if nature were implacable. But it is not. Nature's flexibility tells us that deer and rabbits, palm trees and roses, elephants and several million Jains, will continue to treat the world gently, even if the

Arctic wolves continue to feast on lemmings and mice; even as the African cheetah goes after the gazelle. Nature stipulates a balance in which there are winners and losers, boom and bust, population dynamics encompassing carnage and compassion.

Nature, evolution, is altogether flexible, eager to test new possibilities, to explore new modes of behavior, as it does with its varieties of genetical lineage, its fervent, diversified array of DNA. There is free will in nature, as in human nature. Every ontological argument that has ever been advanced for the existence of god has never solved the dilemma of pain.

The Greeks, Anselm, St. Thomas Aquinas, Albert Schweitzer, have all recognized the vicissitudes, in spite of god. Contrary to evolutionary expectation, the elephant, the gorilla, the rhino, the hippo, the megamouth shark (the largest shark in the world) are all vegetarians, in spite of their size and the human presumption that the mighty need meat. The brontosaurus—the biggest, the mightiest animal that ever lived, and it lived for tens-of-millions of years—was a vegetarian. Human beings have been around for less than 100,000 years. For most of that time, the majority of human food was gathered by women, and it was in the form of pulses, fruits, and vegetables. The male hunters were always on the fringes of obsolete protein.

Others will argue that they simply *crave* the taste of a hamburger once in a while. And since there's no law preventing it, and nobody's looking over their shoulder, they can afford to ignore their conscience for the few minutes that it takes to devour a fast-food lunch. Jains have analyzed those "few minutes" and worked out various meditations and disciplines to avoid such temptation, the same way that "Alcoholics Anonymous," or various drug rehabilitation centers have sought to assist those addicted to harmful toxins. Killing, directly or indirectly, is the worst of all toxins. Not only does it kill a living being, but it inflicts enormous damage on one's own soul, which is the quintessence of all life. The soul itself, say the Jains, is not the one eating the hamburger. The soul is pure. But the physical body and its complex of desires and neuroses attach themselves to the soul, weaken it, obscure its nascent purity, and this process thickens with each needless moment of oblivion, until the soul is virtually snuffed out, mumbling in perdurable darkness, with no one to hear it, and no hope of ever making beautiful music.

Those "few minutes" of psychological impasse, passion, disinterest, oblivion, appetite, are the same few moments that it takes to vent rage, to murder someone, to inflict every pain known to the human arsenal. Those few moments—repeated in so many variations—caused World War I—with its twenty million dead, fifty million injured; and nearly every other violent tantrum and disorder known to the brain. To temper that killer in man, and the subsequent killing fields, is to grope with those few moments where conflict begins.

Two minutes of unthinking, unfeeling behavior: Whether in the eating of a hamburger, the casting of a fishing line, or, more subtly, the habit of taking one's children to a circus to view animals who in fact have been reduced to insanity and pain. Two minutes of our own insanity, in the breeding of captive animals who were meant to be free, or worse—the abandoning of those pets to certain death; in the reining, or worse, the racing of horses; the killing of bugs in a frenzy of vindictiveness, as opposed to more patiently removing them without injury. The litany of transgressions cascades with numbing ubiquity. And it all comes down to the collaboration—mindful or not—with atrocity carried out by, or on behalf of humans, and committed against other living creatures—whether around the dinner table, on the job, on the farm, the ranch, in the street, at the grocery store, in one's financial investments, in the donations one makes (many medical foundations, for example, put their charity dollars towards animal research—animal torture, in other words), in the clothes one wears, and so on.

This is the forlorn syndrome of "two minute" human aggression upon which Jainism has arisen. Desmond Morris describes "the animal contract," a peace treaty with all other life forms which we have forever shunned. In his groundbreaking investigation into biomedical abuse, Hans Ruesch terms this persistent abrogation our "slaughter of the innocent." Meanwhile, the United States Congress heaps all such transgressions and legal evasion under the hopelessly feckless "Animal Welfare Act" of 1964.

And yet, for every outrage, somewhere, there is an equal avowal of conscious restraint, appreciation, love, which brings back to its anonymous donor a blessing, in the end. In our own time, humanitarians like Peter Singer have termed the remedial consciousness "animal liberation." There is no greater lasting source of joy than in the saving of an animal's life; the extending of one's aid to the needy. It is the single-most bulwark against darkness, the force of good that must combat every evil.

Upon this physical, emotive battlefield, otherwise known as paradise, human beings think, dream, and strategize. We can easily change the course of our destiny. We needn't give in to those few minutes of oblivion—of laziness—at the root of our aggression. We can negotiate, talk it out, learn, empathize, crack jokes, simply say no, or simply say yes. For the Jains, "all the evils of the world owe their origin to *Rag* and *Dwesh* (attachment and animosity)."[4] We can satisfy our hunger, our possessiveness and territoriality through means other than Rag and Dwesh, predation and greed. Our grocery stores are brimming as a result of our fourteen-thousand year old agricultural brains, not any so-called hunting instinct. And our art is flourishing, not because we have killed, but because we have loved.

Here, on the printed page, these are merely words, of course. And with so myriad a legacy of pain and horror—as depicted above—enshrouding our best instincts and ideals, there is every reason to doubt the viability of any moral pretense that would grapple after the idea of human sanity or compassion. Indeed, as Nietzsche and so many philosophers have stated resignedly, humans are the most *inhuman* of all animals.

A skeptic—as Sir Arthur Conan Doyle pointed out—is one who feels compelled to count the legs on a centipede. Unapologetic skepticism is easily levied against those who would proffer non-violence. Human history has unrelentingly built up an imposing edifice of evidence to indict *Homo sapiens* in nearly any court of reason. Indeed, according to the most lucid of defense prosecutors, god must surely be dead.

But such skepticism has not had much staying power in the arena of great art. One can not easily uphold cynicism in the presence of a Giorgione, or Vivaldi, or Vermeer. And the reason is, I suspect, that the imagination realigns the soul, steering it clear of the habitual madness that is the mundane, opening up vistas we had forgotten, or ignored, prompting feelings long suppressed, reinstating that dignity which is our true birthright.

Jainism contains the same imaginative prowess as the greatest art. It too is an art form, and it has been termed *ethical realism*.[5] Jainism is the only religion that has no god, and yet is not atheistic. How can that be? In a very telling sense, the Jains have replaced the notion of god, with "the own nature of things" *(vastu-sva-bhavah-dharmah)*. Perhaps that is the secret to their idealism: god has never let them down, has never wavered. Jains are accountable to nature, and thus to themselves, to their families, their community, and to the vast menagerie of life forms which co-inhabit this planet with them. Jainism's accessible genius is this total embrace of the earth—so ancient, so contemporary. One truth being equal to all truths, one organism being equal to all organisms, one square inch of land equal to all land, and all pain requiring serious consideration, any aspect of Jainism thereby reflects the whole. This is its imperative and homeostasis; its first ring of truth. As grounds for a viable ecological contract, Jainism has achieved perfect pitch.

Like an idea, a religious Antarctica, ethics embracing continents, dreams detailed on the horizon, Jainism exists in the realms of the imagination, as much as in reality. The two realms are not dissociated. The idea itself is purifying, restitutional. With discipline, with patience, a Jain can work on his waking life, as on his dreams, to acquit himself of any ill-intentions or deeds, and subsequently manifest that acquittal in the pursuit of his daily bread, his higher goals, and all of his myriad connections.

It is true that Jainism has not stopped violence in the world, though it has gone a long way towards doing so within India. But

Jains themselves are not part of that global problem. They are part of the local solutions. They *are* the solution:

"Ahimsa is freedom from all miseries...To those who aspire for happiness of the Soul, Ahimsa to them is like sky to the birds, water to the thirsty, bread to the hungry, a boat to the drowning, medicine to the sick, and a guide to lost ones in the woods." [6]

Everyone I have ever known who has taken the time to learn about Jainism has become something of a Jain. I truly believe such conversion is unavoidable, not because the Jains teach anything we don't already intimately understand, at least in our hearts, but precisely because they remind us of our own first principles in such a way that we can no longer deny the urgency and beauty of such remembrance. There is great allure in re-calling ourselves, the fascination of an old photograph from childhood. We touch the face, the unwrinkled skin, the fairer hair; the eyes were fresh, no dark circles; the smile seemed as if it knew no beyond, was prepared to smile sheepishly, murmur gingerly, forever; to be good, lodged cozily in Dr. Dolittle's barn, a Puddleby-on-Marsh of universal sensibility. All of our subsequent experiences—the joys, the sorrows—are instantly compressed into the glimpse backwards. Our inner nature calls to us like a photograph from the Arcadia of our beginnings. We do not merely carry that photograph in our wallet. We harbor it in our *being*—not the philosophical being of a Wittgenstein or Heidegger, but the wonderment, innocence, and joy of childhood.

But Jainism is not about fairy tales or returning to simplicity. It is about safeguarding our roots, becoming adults, acting responsibly. Our photographs from childhood should give us hope, strength, the willpower to insist on the nature which is in us. Idle hopes? Far-off dreams?

There are, as one would expect, vulnerable nuances throughout Jain thinking, largely on account of the vulnerability of any organism, particularly one that thinks about itself. I have not felt the need to dwell upon those nuances—what some might call hypocrisy, weakness, contradiction. We know that life is contradictory, that any system of thought and belief is prey to inconsistency, daunting rules, lists—ENDLESS LISTS—of vows, sanctions, transgressions, injunctions. People can not live by lists. I have known at least one member of a Jain family who secretly ate meat; and another one who—not so secretly—sported leather shoes. But what has stood out in Jainism for me—beyond the hierarchy of details, is not its few imperfections, or academic bent, but its penetrating insights, phenomenal integrity, and child-like idealism—unblushing, naked, powerful, and enduring. It is the unique *ideal* of Jainism that I have herewith endeavored to convey. That ideal is the most sublime and important message ever conceived by our species, in my opinion. It is like a telegram from the earth herself.

Many have previously opened that telegram and read it aloud. Non-violence has long been consciously pursued by dozens of tribal and religious groups, as well as individual thinkers, from Christ to the Physicians for Social Responsbility. Today, anthropologists know of numerous relatively non-violent cultures, like the sixty or so Tasaday of the southern Philippines who nurture consistent respect for life, as opposed to aggression. One could cite the Tahitians, the Tanzanian Hadza, the West Malaysian Semai, the Qipisamiut Eskimos, Australian Murngin and Walbiri, the Rajasthani Bishnoi, Bolivian Quollayuaha, and the Ituri Pygmies. By relative standards, these last remaining outposts of minimalist infliction remind us of our essentially utopian past, where we took only what was needed, and nothing in excess.[7] Such few remaining tribes eke out their livelihood according to a massively ecological instinct of resource management, biological carrying capacity, and sustainable harvest.[8]

From the Jain point of view, such ethnographic examples are fraught with problems which would suggest that the 'noble savage' is a myth. The Pygmies brutally assault elephants, the Eskimos kill walrus and whales, the oceanic islanders that so entranced Margaret Mead have not been immune to the battle cry, and slaughter fish daily, while the forty-thousand year old Australian aborigines feed upon hundreds of species of animals and insects. The Jains expect much more from human beings than convenient, easy slaughter. Strikingly, Jains do not worship nature, nor harbor any particular romance of the wilderness, and thus they are not led astray by the simplistic picture of man in nature that has fueled so much western, and oriental mysticism. Jains are almost entirely urban oriented. Of the above-mentioned tribes, only the Bishnoi come close to realizing the spiritual biology of Jainism, despite the fact that the Bishnoi keep cattle. There may be a good reason for this similarity: the Bishnoi could well have inherited their deep-seated cultural aversion to aggression from the Jains, some of whom, for many centuries, have co-existed along side the Bishnoi in Rajasthan.

As an idea in history, pure non-violence—that of the Bishnoi shepherd with his flock, surviving on the proverbial grapes, olives, bread, wine and milk products—can be traced from the earliest nature writings of men like Lucretius, the Desert Fathers, the Egyptian Khety, the Greek and Roman Thales and Plotinus, through the Middle Ages Asiatic visions of poets and painters such as Han Shan, Kuo Hsi, and Li Ch'eng, as well as the Renaissance master of Persia, Sultan-Muhammed. The vision of nature perceived in the ancient Near East, in China, Japan and Tibet was largely the product of a non-violent sensibility. But it was a minority opinion. While it can be argued that the Southern and Northern Sung Dynasties, with their animistic Taoism, showed a marked reverence for nature, such inclinations were not practiced by a popularist movement in China. And in Japan, where the Zen Buddhists interpreted those Chinese Taoist canons, such love of nature did not prevent Japanese Buddhism from embarking on a notoriously violent path for many centuries. Zen priests waged wars, and the repeated carnage perpetrated by monks atop sacred Mount Hiei (above Kyoto) always stood out as a bloody blight on the otherwise tranquil musings of Buddhism.

Even Himalayan Buddhism, the penultimate reservoir of non-violence, could not neutralize the importunate Chinese avalanche that has thrown Tibetan tranquility into disarray. Obviously, this was not Tibetan Buddhism's fault, but it shows how vulnerable non-violence is.

Such contradictions in the west are too numerous to detail here, though certain highlights are worth remembering. In *The Suppliants*, Euripides had asked, "Why does war ever have to break out...Leave others in peace. Life is short." Aristophanes, too, sought alternatives to the massive violence demonstrated by the Peloponnesian War. His Athenian farmer, Dikaiopolis, hero of his play *Acharnians* took refuge far from the military realities of his time to live peacefully and privately according to a strategy ignored by other Greeks. In *Lysistrata*, the women refused sex to their husbands until a lasting peace could be achieved with Athen's enemies. In reality, the Treaty of Nicias was hammered out, as reflected in Aristophanes's play, *Peace*. But a few years later, Greece was once again involved in war. The Sicilian expedition saw fifty thousand young men needlessly perish.

In early Christianity, Christ was pronounced the Prince of Peace and the early Donatist and Pelagian pacifists recommended aversion to war, a state of benevolent nature looked over by angels. St. Augustine analyzed warring behavior in his *Contra Faustum*, and argued that certain wars were just and that those killed by good Christian soldiers would in any event have been killed for their sins by God. This was surely the logic underlying the Crusaders's religious zeal, however distantly removed from the original love psalms of Jesus Christ.

The contradictions emerged in Rome, as well, an empire with an unprecedented record of violence. Yet, along the Mysian coast in northwestern Asia Minor, lived a tribe of people opposed to all war, vegetarians, said to exist in a pure state of nature. This early anthropological oddity inspired Virgil in his *Georgics*, as well as Lucretius, both of whom celebrated restrained, rural life.[9]

Yet specifically pacifist doctrine in the West was uncommon before the Waldensian movement in southern France during the twelfth century. Anabaptists promoted non-violence during the Reformation as did the Mennonites, though many were to end up in Oliver Cromwell's Model Army. Quakers too have taken up arms at various times, though their creed is one of passive resistance, best epitomized by William Penn's unarmed settlement in the colony of Pennsylvania. The Plymouth Brethren and the Christadelphians refused to bear arms, and numerous elements in Judaism, Methodism, and Roman Catholicism have opted for conscientious objection during wartime.

Men like Hugo Grotius, Shogun Ieyasu, Immanuel Kant and Woodrow Wilson have proposed enlightened antidotes to human aggression. Yet in spite of such reasoned approaches to moderation, by world-renowned thinkers, politicians have gone on to engage their contingents in more than 250,000 major battles since the time of the Renaissance; one hundred million dead from war in the twentieth century alone; not a single decade in American history, for example, when U.S. troops were not somewhere engaged in armed conflict.[10]

In Renaissance Europe, the devotion to Greco-Roman themes —Arcadia, the pasturalist vision, landscape poetry and painting— hinged, once again, on aesthetic refinements, schools of cultivation which were not mainstream ways of life. One would be hard pressed to argue the case of a "Leonardo-factor" altering the way in which sixteenth century Italians lived, for example. Indeed, much of Renaissance art's pastoral legacy grew out of the sickening disruptions of daily life occasioned by nearly constant warfare. It was Leonardo, remember, who invented the first practical submarine which he offered to the Venetians for their many battles against the Pope, Genoa, and the Turks. The sublime art of a Sannazaro, a Giorgione, or a Monteverdi did not have much apparent influence upon the aggressive behavior of Renaissance life.

But in India, a country that has been no stranger to violence, Jainism absolutely changed the course of a sub-continent. Its aesthetic principles altered the mindset, religious devotion, and daily life of tens-of-millions. Jain intellectualism impacted on the common man. It is an arguable point among scholars, yet there is good reason to reflect that six-hundred million Hindus today trace their orthodoxy—with its own reverence for life and stated vegetarianism—not to Brahmanic, but rather sramanic tradition, namely, to the ancient Jain ascetics whose sculptured remnants have turned up in the archeological fields of the Indus Valley civilizations.

(Keep in mind that not all Hindus—by any means—are vegetarians, any more than Buddhists are. Jains constitute what is the only major religion in the world that is unconditionally vegetarian.)

It has been theorized that the images from Mohenjodaro of the naked yogis reflect a pattern that would be repeated later on in Jain sculpture.[11]

The importance of these findings goes a long way towards certifying the pre-Aryan, pre-Vedic inroads of Jainism across Asia. Professor A. Chakravarti has suggested that the Harappa and Mohenjodaro figures of the Yogi and the bull indicate a connection with the very first Tirthankara, Rishabha (or Adinatha), and a "cult of ahimsa" which was the faith of those residents of the early Indus valley.[12]

The archeological record is also interesting from another point of view: Jainism has evolved. While no weapons from the period of the Indus River Valley cultures have ever been found—reaffirming the "cult of ahimsa" theory, of an entire civilization devoted to non-violence—Rishabha's supposed teachings with respect to the domestication of animals and the use of bulls in agriculture, would later be rejected as the antipathy of true ahimsa.

Buddhism itself voices its indebtedness to this evolving Jainism. There are hundreds-of-millions of Buddhists in the world today. The Jains arguably prompted the Buddhist calling. Mahavira (also called Vardhamana, 599-527 B.C.), the twenty-fourth *Tirthankara* (path-finder, ford-maker) or *jina* (sage, literally, forger of the stream, spiritual victor, conqueror of self) was an elder contemporary of Buddha (567-487). While the two men did not apparently know one another, there is sufficient documentation to assert that Buddha initially studied under later disciples of Parshva, the twenty-third Tirthankara, Mahavira's predecessor by two-hundred-fifty years (877-777 B.C.). Buddhist scriptures refer to Mahavira as the Nigantha Nataputta, an ascetic preaching the old dharma. Jain scriptures do not apparently mention Buddha.

Whatever Buddha's original feelings with respect to Parshva, Buddhists themselves are not consistently vegetarians[13]; nor do they go out of their way to safeguard animals, or actively protect the environment, in spite of a long tradition of nature reverence, and a resurgence of contemporary Buddhist activism.[14] The nature-based philosophies of Buddhism, while promoting a love of the wilderness and a passionate belief in the interdepended-ness of all beings, nevertheless stumble over the issue of meat-eating, which is tantamount, for the Jains, to collapsing the whole position in supposed defense of nature. With this in mind, it is worth remembering that when Mahavira delivered his first sermon, his congregation was called *Samavasarana* precisely because the word refers to an equality of religious opportunity for all creatures, great and small, animal and human-animal.[15] There is always a place for animals in the Jain temples. Moreover, legend has it that Mahavira's vernacular was understandable to all species.

Buddhism holds that what will be will be, an easy way of saying that the wheel of life is ineluctable. Moreover, many Buddhists will claim that the Buddhist meat eater is facilitating the animal corpse's speedy reincarnation into human form, and thus expediting its chances at attaining nirvana. This doctrine was explained to me by a young reincarnate lama in Kathmandu, and I have heard it reiterated countless times by other Buddhists in Nepal, India, China, Japan and Tibet. In numerous Himalayan Buddhist monasteries, I have seen monks routinely serving meat to each other. Hindus are equally inconstant with respect to this flesh-bound dharma. It is destiny, they say. However, Buddhists absolutely forbid the actual killing of an animal. In Tibet, there is a caste of specifically chosen "untouchable" types, who may gather up the remains of animals that have met natural ends, and feed such meat to the Buddhists, in the form, for example, of a yak stew. Some might argue that this is merely passing the buck.

"Jainas became the primary exponents of vegetarianism in India," writes Professor Jaini.[16] "They rejected even the Buddhist notion that meat is acceptable if an animal has died of natural causes, contending that the dead flesh itself is a breeding ground for innumerable nigodas and hence must not be consumed."

Brahmchari Sital Prashad has taken up this controversy by examining the old Sanskrit and Pali texts pertaining to the striking similarities between the two religions. Citing the *Lankavatara Sutra's* eighth chapter, Prashad points to passages that clearly resolve whatever ambiguities may surround Buddha's own alleged acceptance of meat:

"In this beginningless world the living beings having been wandering, there is not a single creature which had not been sometimes mother, father, brother, sister, son, daughter or any other relative. The same adopting many re-births, are born as deer or other animal, bird etc. which are really our relatives. How can a follower of Buddhism, a saint or a disciple, who sees all the creatures as his brethren, cut the flesh of all these creatures?"[17]

Despite such commentary, Buddhists are not, as a rule, vegetarians. To eat the meat is to break the contract, the promise of commiseration. Without this most simple of restraints, no symbol, no supposed summons of the spirit, can be easily trusted. The idea of consuming an animal is nearly as horrific to the Jains as the act of murder itself. In no other religion have thought and action been so intricately merged, a unity of behavior, and an environmental code of ethics that permeates every aspect of Jain life, posterity, and history.

CHAPTER TWO

First Encounters

SOME YEARS AGO while travelling through West-Central India I came across a temple marked by immaculately-clean spires of gleaming white marble. I was unfamiliar with the sanctuary, having studied Vedic and Buddhist traditions in northern India and the Himalayas for a few years, but knowing next to nothing about the Jains. I walked to the entrance of this monastic complex only to be scrutinized by an apparent attendant. He asked me, somewhat apologetically, if I might not remove my watch. I assumed it was because such monasteries adhered only to celestial time, *kalpas* measured in tens-of-thousands of human years, rather than the mundane fixation with watches and schedules.

I was mistaken, however. My watch was off-limits because of its leather band. This was a Jain temple. To enter Jain space wearing any animal product—leather watchband, leather belt, suede shoes, leather jacket, etc.—would be unthinkable.

I could have eaten off the floor of the temple, its smooth, white marble slabs were so impeccably polished and clean. Every square inch of the courtyards and columns had been carved, chiselled, moulded with patience and love and symbolism that yielded a picture of the world quite unlike the Hindu and Buddhist pantheons to which I was more accustomed, such as battle scenes from the *Mahabharata* and *Ramayana* epics. Or pious monks paying obeisance to their heavenly Buddhist deities who descended from mandara nirvanas to lead the worshipful into one Pure Land or another.

These Jain carvings bore no resemblance to such far-away incitements. They seemed rather down-to-earth, instead. And it must be admitted that the cleanliness of the temple was also altogether distinct from the malodorous taint of so many non-Jain temples that I have encountered across Asia.

With its uncanny calm, and silent coolness, I had the sensation of being totally sheltered from the world. It is the same feeling I've had in certain English country gardens. Nor was there the slightest sense of monastic authority; no regal chambers, hidden administrative labyrinths; no imposing corridors leading to abbatial cloisters or inner sanctums. All was as it appeared—glistening, marble sages whose names or significance were as yet unknown to me, sculpted in the shadowed eaves of downsloping ceilings. Nary another visitor. Only parrots cooing in the polished alcoves, and a white-faced, unassuming monkey perched contemplatively along one of many walls.

I sat for an hour or so wondering why I seemed to be alone in this perfect hiatus of time, a hewn marvel of primeval sensibility, surrounded by the nude statuary and benevolent faces of immaculate white stone, eyes of blue lapis or black onyx. No voices calling to me. No cacophony produced by human thigh bones. But rather, the collusion of poetic peace and rational space. No semblance of mystique, as is so easily summoned in, say, a high Tibetan or Nepalese monastery. Again, something else entirely: a conjuration hopelessly out of tune with the passions, such as they are in India. There was the kind of eccentricity that surfaces throughout one's life and calls into question every other query; tells us, like a knowing deja-vu, that we need search no farther. The search itself expends too much precious energy. There are more important things to be done, this poignancy of inner space seems to suggest.

I was intrigued by this first encounter. The temple guardian turned out to be a mere visitor like myself, on pilgrimage from the Punjab. He was dressed in a white, two-piece sarong, of sorts, barefooted, his head shaved, he seemed supremely at peace, collected. He'd done me a favor by bidding me to remove my leather articles. As we spoke, I learned that he was a Shvetambara (white-robed) renunciate, a former businessman who had finally taken vows, *diksha* (initiation), and was embarking on the life of a Jain ascetic, having reached the grand old age of sixty.

In Jainism, there are two types of devotees—lay votaries, who observe the small vows (*anuvratas*) and must live their lives in constant moderation, and the ascetics who practice the great vows *(mahavratas)* and live lives totally focused on self-control. Such control implies the absolute limiting of one's desires *(iccha-parimana)* and of one's possessions (*parigraha-parimana).* But that was just the beginning, as I would later learn. Alteration of thinking and of behavior is what constituted true Jainism. This man had made the apparent transition from small vows to great vows. Accordingly, his normal day would have been divided into four parts: in the morning he would study, then meditate, then go begging, and finally, before darkness, he would study again.[18]

A few years later I would find myself sitting with Ram Suriji, the leader of India's more than seven million Shvetambara Jains. At the time he was ninety-two years old, propped up in bed in the rear room of a large suburban way station for pilgrims. He had traveled much of his life from village to village. Infirm, he was at that time carried by his many monk compatriots. In a few days, he and the hundreds of other monks in his company would be back out on the road, sleeping at other such urban campsites, giving vows to their multitude of lay adherents. Ram Suriji had never allowed himself to be photographed before that day, according to his assistants, believing that artificial lights, i.e. a flash, killed organisms. However, he made an exception for me and my film crew because he said that he was very old and wanted to inform the world of *ahimsa*, before it was too late.

I'll never forget his pained, sincere description of his faith (herewith, an exact transcription):

"In all life, whether it is the human, animal kingdom, or other kingdom, no one would like to suffer. You would not like to suffer. You would not like to suffer by others's bad deeds. Neither we would like to suffer. So all the life—whether insect, animal kingdom or other kingdom, nobody would like to suffer. Even when we walk we can't," (he paused, trying to be precise, to clarify) "we have to walk by looking on the ground. We cannot cook. We cannot keep any money. We have to go out and beg from different houses and acquire only a small portion of the food prepared for themselves that they should not suffer. That they should not give more than what is necessary."

Later, speaking with another young Shvetambara, I was told, "We are in constant touch with the common people, barefoot, walking, trying to eliminate all violence. To live honestly with life. That is ahimsa."

I was swayed by these men. Such ascetics remain only a day or two in any one village, except during the monsoon, when they are at rest for a few months. They do not wander during the rainy season on account of the profusion of bugs and frogs that live in the water and the mud. Despite all of the monks' precautions, not walking anywhere until they clearly see the road in front of them, they would still invariably step on a bug, if during monsoon, thus violating their most basic, heartfelt preamble. Their every minute, conscious as well as unconscious, is concerned with one guiding mandate, which is ahimsa.

I learned that the monks were indeed wholly dependent upon lay followers. This dependency enforces an extraordinary relationship: Jain ascetics are essentially urban. They need to be with other people, who in turn need to secure their own religious vows.

These monks were the ultimate symbols of gentleness, never imposing, never interfering. Simply trying to let nature be, they walk, spreading the message of peace from village to village.

Following the doctrines of their twenty-four revered sages (Mahavira most prominently), the Jains are remarkable for their ability to have made a modern success story out of ancient religious beliefs. Pre-dating both Hindus and Buddhists, the Jains today constitute one percent of the Indian population. And yet, Jains are said to contribute a proportionately considerable share of all Indian philanthropic donations. Their money comes predominately from environmentally sound, non-violent occupations—banking, real estate, diamonds, pawning, computer technology, law and adjudication, accounting, medicine, government positions, publishing, teaching, ecological science, aesthetics, astronomy, physics and engineering. The Jains—who are some of the world's leading pragmatists—have found that non-violence can also be economically fruitful.

This revelation is borne of an ethical approach to all kindred life forms that was to have a transforming effect on Mahatma Gandhi. Gandhi's earliest mentor, and later, his closest friend, were both Jain masters. It was through such tutelage that Gandhi would later effectively argue in a famous letter that it would be preferable to be killed by a snake than to kill the snake. If you must fight, he argued, then fight with non-violence.

"If ahimsa be not the law of our being, then my whole argument falls to pieces," he would write.

Whoever would doubt the viability of such a philosophy need only turn to its stubborn triumph as realized against the British rule in India.

For the Jain, all animal life is inviolate. Every organism possesses a soul, known as *jiva*, from a minute amoeba virus, to the enormous redwood tree with its 36,000 cubic feet of life. That soul is independent, endowed with a strong personality and individual destiny. Every organism is capable of achieving salvation, happiness, and must be allowed to continue on its path. This universal respect is no mere gesture. Jainism pays no tribute to lip service. The Digambara Jains are distinguished by naked monks who brush the ground before them with peacock feathers whenever they sit down, making sure that no bugs or other living things are accidentally injured. Some Jain monks wear masks to protect insects from flying in their mouths and being killed there. All Jain mendicants are forbidden the use of artificial lights, or flying in airplanes, or riding in trains or automobiles. Once again, the rationale is based upon a strict unwillingness to engage in any activity that might inadvertently crush a blade of grass, or harm an organism likely to be flattened beneath a tire, or sucked into a turbo-engine.

These are only some of the more visible habits characteristic of a people whose shyness and peacefulness are legendary. They do not proselytize and have thus attracted very few outsiders to their way of life. Indeed, until the late nineteenth century, Jains preferred not to show their manuscripts to non-Jains and for this reason Jainism remained virtually unknown outside of India, or confused as a sub-sect of Hinduism, or of Buddhism. Jainism was not discovered by foreigners until the late eighteenth century, when a group of English Indologists first began publishing accounts of the religion as an altogether separate cultural and spiritual phenomenon of monumental importance. Subsequently, a number of French and German scholars throughout the nineteenth and early twentieth centuries made enormous strides in attempting to understand this religion whose antiquity was soon seen to be greater, even, than Buddhism; and whose way of life appeared absolutely undiluted from the times of its earliest sages.[19]

What is the Jain way of life? Most Jains do not wander the backroads naked, wearing masks over their mouths, refraining from modern means of travel. But all Jains are strict vegetarians. The Jains long ago developed a distinctive science of botany that recognized a subtle and sophisticated web of sensation in the natural world. That translates into a world which feels everything. Lettuce feels; elephants feel; people feel. Feelings, in turn, can be categorized according to their intensity. Lettuce, rhubarb, and other vegetables possess one sense organ, say the Jains. People, generally speaking, possess five sense organs. The Jains allow themselves to consume only those creatures with no more than one sense organ. And even this life-saving habit of minimalist consumption is undertaken with a degree of modesty and embarrassment.

Even so, the Jains discourage farming because it so often inflicts unnecessary pain upon animals. Jains keep no pets. And in a country noted for its veneration of cows, the Jains worship no animal, no god, no divine being. Worship—say the Jains—is a form of interference. Love can also interfere, they go on, as when the passions are enflamed, then misdirected, or turned against the object of their desire. Ahimsa is about minimizing pain and thus minimizing the passions, all except the passion for alleviating pain itself. This is the one contradictory tautology that Jains embrace. They express love, naturally, as human beings. But they are also vigilant with respect to its dark side. The monks have called for love. But they have done so carefully. There are no virgins on the altar, in Jainism. No neurotic feminism, or male chauvinism; no rape; no sexual abuse. Love is pure in this religion among equals.

Lest this strike the non-Jain as hopelessly conservative, or boring, in a world that could do well to multiply its kisses and love affairs, one need only consider the erotic sculpture that graces the exteriors of so many Jain temples. In some instances the sculpted passions are wild and orgiastic, like those at Khajuraho and the temple of Taranga. Yet these procreative juices of stone flow only on the outside of the sanctuaries. Once the pilgrim enters the inner world of devout Jainism, he or she leaves those impulses behind.

It is this same love, these same tenets, that enact other devout forms of behavior. For example, the Jains prescribe no drugs that derive from animal products. At one Jain medical facility that I had the opportunity to visit, human immuno-globulin was being produced. Rabbits were being tested, then released back out into the wild. In most (non-Jain) laboratories, rabbits are killed once they have been used, and re-used. Among the Jains, never. The owner of this establishment, a doctor, took me aside, however, and confessed to his deeper troubles. He knew that the keeping of rabbits was sinful, even though they were ultimately released, and in spite of the fact that the end-result of their service would aid in the treatment of diseases. It was my first taste of an idealism shot through with partiality. I expected to find numerous other instances where theory typically broke down in practice. But I did not.

Because they emphasize the minimizing of pain as a condition of being truly human, the Jains have tended towards consistently rational, if not progressive points of view.

Jainism was the only large-scale force in Indian society that never accepted the caste system, and that provided equal status and equal rights to women. Those rights—however restrictive in their definition—included abortion, and while the fetus is considered inviolate from the moment of conception, the lay Jains—conscious of population control—allow for medically approved forms of birth control. This is not to suggest that the Jain *religion* officially ordains contraception, but as a social practice it is allowed. In addition, a Jain doctor will normally agree to perform an abortion if the mother's health is in jeopardy.

I met with a physician who had specialized in tropical medicine and ran a Jain ashram in Gujarat. His goal, in company with students and colleagues who came for meditation and discussion, was to see how the practice of ahimsa could best address and solve such age-old human concerns as abortion and euthanasia.

"It all depends on the point of view," he began. "You cannot kill a live human being. But, again, it depends upon the individual. Not all can take a spiritual attitude....The inconveniences to the mother (must be taken into consideration). From a medical point of view, termination of pregnancy is desirable, either for the health of the mother, or because of the abnormalities forming in the fetus. In such cases, medical termination of pregnancy is accepted on both medical and ethical grounds as well."

As for capital punishment, Jains vehemently oppose it. I had the good fortune to visit with one of India's leading constitutional lawyers who summarized his views this way:

"I will perhaps opt for a particular point of view because I am influenced by the Jain philosophy of life. Take for example capital punishment. I'm opposed to it. I might have been opposed to it even if I were not a Jain. But perhaps it is quite possible that I'm opposed to it because I've grown up with this whole philosophy of life which rejects brutalizations of man, which rejects violence as an instrument of achieving the goal and that does not regard violence as a value in itself—even if it is committed by the state."

Euthanasia, however, is considered by most Jains (the Terapanthi sect excluded) to be justifiable. Here again, practical, empathetic concerns take priority over the doctrine of non-interference.

Pharmaceuticals deriving from animal products, bio-medical research, the hotel business (when non-vegetarian food is involved), industrial agricultural or logging interests, are all forbidden.

The only form of self-willed death that is ever sanctioned is the one ritual practice of *sallekhana* whereby a Jain mendicant fasts to death in a state of profound meditation under the following circumstances: 1) it must be a terminal illness or involve the loss of a vital organ or appendage that would keep the mendicant from adhering to a vow; and it must be medically certain that his death is fast approaching; 2) it is done in public under the supervision of the monk's teachers and a minimum of five people present; 3) the fasting vows are taken for the duration of twenty-fours only. Thus the option to start eating again is always easily renewed, should the mendicant change his or her mind. Sallekhana is never a private act.

In the rural town of Kanor, where several hundred *Terapanthi* (a relatively modern sub-sect of the Sthanakavasi-Shvetambara) monks and nuns had convened for a few days, I met with their spiritual leader, Acarya Tulsi. He presided over a group of disciples whose white garb and masks were spectacular against the burnished hot sky. I'd seen them earlier that day, wandering barefooted along the two-lane country rode, past endless expanses of wild mustard flowers. They presented a countenance of supreme elegance centuries old. But the Terapanthi are not focused on the past. Their concerns, voiced to me by Acarya Tulsi, are totally of the moment:

"Not only must we condemn all research in atomic weaponry, which is itself violence, but we must experiment with ahimsa, training people who will practice ahimsa. We have established institutes where students are actively studying peace. And while the west is busy experimenting with violence, we are experimenting with non-violence. This is our belief. This is our message for the west, for the whole world."

Acarya Tulsi's nun counterpart, Sister Kanakaprabha, was seated with dozens of her compatriots. She added, "Our nuns are working with women of all religions throughout the country to help them break the shackles of oppression which are so rampant in this male-dominated country of India."

It is interesting to observe that there has not been a single legal proceeding involving a Terapanthi "as plaintiff, defendant, complainant, or accused, or even as a witness"—in the nearly 225 years of the sect's existence.[20]

In every Jain village and major city throughout India, animal sanctuaries can be found. These veterinarian oases, known as *panjorapors* are supported by Jain, and sometimes Hindu, donations. Stray animals—birds, camels, water buffalo, cows, etc.—are brought in, cared for, loved, and visited at least once a week by veterinarians. At one bird sanctuary in downtown New Delhi, adjoining the Digambara Temple, I witnessed some thirty thousand parrots and pigeons being fed by a handful of erstwhile Jain volunteers. In Bombay, hidden in the heart of a busy market, I visited another panjorapor. Children would come to fondle the aging cattle that had been collected from off the streets, where their fate was typically to wander until they were old, incapable of giving milk, and thus condemned to a miserable slow starvation.

The Jains are aghast at such cruel twists of fate. They perceive human beings as a collective island of faith, a bastion of conscience harboring the mechanism for spreading comfort amongst all such living creatures. As one more species, we may indulge in self-serving soliloquy down through biological history, but if we have taken nature seriously, studied her ill-winds, considered our own spectacular possibilities, then we will ultimately agree on compassion; the singular capacity for healing a wounded world. We are the remedy. We need only recognize it. I saw dozens of rescued cows, some with gauze pads affixed to injuries; and a hobbling camel with a splint on one leg. A little girl kissing a bull. An old woman with a bucket of grain for stray egrets.

Such beneficence is not witheld from human animals, to be sure. The Jains have built hospitals and schools all over India to help India's ailing, and to educate the young people on issues pertaining to child abuse, wife beating, animal cruelty, ecology, vegetarianism, and the nuclear arms race.

At the Sarvodaya Hospital outside of Bombay, the Jains have funded cancer and TB wards. Sri Chitrabhanu, a former Jain monk who walked in the traditional manner throughout India for twenty years, was instrumental in developing Sarvodaya. I followed him during one of his frequent visits to the hospital. Every day, thousands of lame, homeless and diseased come to this institution for Jain medical assistance. Chitrabhanu—a prolific author—was there blessing and comforting these multifarious victims of life.

In Ahmedabad, I encountered a wandering Jain ascetic who had stopped in town for a few days to deliver a speech to the press condemning Star Wars. This young, wild-looking monk spoke half-a-dozen languages, had his Ph.D. in Sanskrit literature from a University in Varanasi, and had already walked barefoot over 100,000 kilometers across India, by his own estimates, spreading the message of ahimsa.

I heard such pleas for peace coming from every corner of the Jain community—from an art historian, a doctor, a wealthy engineer, a poet, a female manufacturer of radiators, the head of a council on world religions, and from a designer of synthetic fabrics. This latter gentleman and his son, followers of Acarya Tulsi's Terapanthi sect, upon learning that tens-of-thousands of silk worms are boiled alive during the normal process of sericulture, has adopted attractive alternatives for his clients. What all of these Jain men and women had in common was an intense belief in non-violence, love of animals, and the message of ahimsa.

The manufacturer of radiators spoke to me from her apartment in Bombay, overlooking the sea. This vital and lovely woman employed several hundred people. She explained that her being raised a Jain had most assuredly transformed her understanding of labor relations. How was that so, I asked her? She then pointed to the leaf of a large plant in her living room. There was a mite, worthy of discussion. Such mites, she said, were carefully scooped up every day with a palm frond, and put outside in the garden. She treated the mites with respect, and showed me precisely what she meant.

This woman—enormously wealthy, but accustomed to sleeping on the hard floor as her nightly austerity *(tapas)*—gently removed the organisms from a leaf with her fingertips, placed them in her palm, walked out into the hall to the elevator in her building, we rode the elevator down to the garden in back, where she then deposited the little creatures in the soil. Simple.

Within a square mile of her apartment complex, I could have counted thousands of less well-off individuals, many living on the fringes of human subsistence. Was it contradictory that this industrialist should spend ten minutes saving a mite, whilst ignoring the starving masses? I asked her, not to bait her, or imply a cruel irony, but to earnestly solicit her opinion on a subject of universal interest.

She was no Mother Theresa. And if the truth be known, Mother Theresa has not exactly solved the problem of India's starving masses, any more than one Digambara industrialist. The Jains say that no individual should interfere in another's life; that absolute non-interference is the beginning of compassion. This sequence of events may seem cockeyed. We are so conditioned to thinking in terms of Peace Corps analogies; peace-keeping forces; the Red Cross; Amnesty International; Greenpeace; People for the Ethical Treatment of Animals; Earth First!; Green parties; the World Wildlife Fund; the Nature Conservancy; of organizations, political movements and individuals who stick their necks out in order to save an animal, preserve a community, or spare an entire ecosystem. The Jains have *quietly* infiltrated politics within India, placing judges in supreme positions, enacting animal legislation in various state governments, and serving on many levels to help resolve national conflicts.

But as individuals, their greatest achievement has been to foster an orthodoxy with respect to all animal life. No one person is perceived as being responsible for the whole world, but rather for that one person's own soul. A soul nurtures itself through compassion. Compassion knows no bounds, as the individual continually enhances his or her range of effectiveness. Jainism promotes a constant expansion of the limits of empathy. Step by step; day by day; at each instance, at every new opportunity. Jainism is not about miracles, or heroism, but practical solutions. The first solution takes place in an individual's soul, the most perilous of battlefields. And while any discussion of soul, and soul-satisfaction, is likely to suggest a form of narcissism, the Jains know that souls are in communication; that all souls are alike; and that until you have your own inner house in order, there is no point trying to save your neighbor. If you can reach out to a simple mite with compassion, it is a small leap to care for several hundred employees.

I visited the industrialist's factory and found a spotless environment, well-paid employees, all of them endowed with unusually lavish benefits and profit sharing plans.

"As a woman industrialist," she began, "the principles that I follow have helped me a great deal: in my interpersonal relationship with my family, with the employees of my company and also with the outside world with which I am associated, to a great extent. I will not spend my money or my company's money which I am running on things which kill. Jainism teaches that all life is equal and therefore I do tend to look at even an ant as an equal to me."

The Jains are not merely unique in their treatment of employees and ants. For this is the only religion in India that has never acknowledged a caste system. Furthermore, the Jains have never contributed to any inequality between the sexes. (Though some Jains chuckled at my western naivety, indicating that I had developed blinders with respect to Jains, thinking they do no wrong; that in fact Jain women were waging their own uphill battle, like women in every country. I suspect, though cannot prove, that Jain women—in general—fare infinitely better than women of other faiths within India, as long as they seek employment within the Jain community). Yet it is clear from the Jain scriptures, that the condition of the sexes is the condition of the Earth, to which Jains are impressively attuned.

I later met with the elegant and understated publisher of the *Times of India*. I noticed as many women as men inhabiting the hundreds of cubicles at the company's downtown New Delhi headquarters. His own office was furnished with volumes of Jain ethical and artistic history, as well as photographs conveying his own devotion to the Digambara sect of Jainism.

Later, at this publisher's home, I feasted on some of the finest Punjabi Jain cuisine imaginable and had the opportunity to view an impressive collection of Jain manuscript illuminations and sculpture. One whole wall was given over to a medieval manuscript (the *Kalpasutra)* with its gorgeous and delicate paintings describing the life of Mahavira and the rules specific to Jain monks during the monsoon period.

With a sweet lassi (yoghurt drink) in his hand, my host talked candidly about his religion:

"Because the way of non-violence is so ingrained in our faith, the business choices—like the fisheries, or the leather business, or an industry where the raw material is of meat, or flesh, was always out to begin with. We never even thought about it. But when the question of the hotel business came in, it was a difficult choice, because we knew that it was a profitable business. We knew that there is alot of money in this business. But because it involves serving of non-vegetarian food to our guests, and making a profit out of it, that's when it was out. We even debated whether we should lease out the restaurant but then we thought that because of making money out of the restaurant, we would still be making money out of non-vegetarian food. So we said that we would not do it."

When he was not at work, or at home, the *Times of India* publisher—like the Digambara radiator industrialist in Bombay—could frequently be found wandering with his teacher, the spiritual head of all Digambara*s*. I followed that teacher one morning to a temple on the outskirts of the city of Indore. There, the late middle-aged naked monk was fed by disciples, then spoke to about forty school children who sat in a circle around him outside. Behind the gathering stood a large naked statue of an enlightened Jain sage. The children exhibited no particular amazement at seeing a naked man talking to them. Not a single giggle; no evidence of confusion or embarrassment. They had grown up thinking of naked monks as the most normal and venerated of adults, exemplars whom their parents admired. India is a country where nude monks have been educating the lay populace for millennia.

He began to speak in a firm and easy style, seated akimbo, his little broom of peacock feathers to his side.

"Twenty-two years ago I took the vow of nudity. Extraordinary as it may appear to you, nudity has become natural to us... We do not possess anything whatsoever and we do not have to tell people to likewise give up their worldly possessions. Our example itself conveys the fact that here is a man who can be happy without having or wanting anything." (He smiled and his eye caught my eye. The contagion of his words had already impressed me to a great extent. The thought of his total freedom, unencumbered self, impassioned disinterest, all set my own heart pounding. I wanted that freedom.) "It is important to see that what hurts himself also must hurt others and what gives happiness to others alone can give happiness to himself. It is ahimsa that makes for friendship between father and son, and love between husband and wife. With these words I bless you. May the whole world remain in peace."[21]

He'd spoken of love, of family. His ultimate asceticism—the living, breathing embodiment, for example, of a St. Francis—did not in the least affect his ability to commend the ordinary connections which most people assert to be the basis of their being. Yet he had converted those passions into an ascetic imperative with respect to non-violence. And he had done so with no particular linguistic prestidigitation, no hat-trick or subtlety. His clarity was empowering. It made enormous sense. The publisher of the *Times of India* had obviously translated such ancient, affable impulses into another kind of success story, that of a prosperous, non-violent business.

I later met another successful Jain businessman. He was said to control a billion-rupee Jain trust for the construction and preservation of temples. A graduate of Harvard University, he had departed from traditional Jain practice by developing one of India's most successful wheat-harvesting operations. Speaking from the living room of his formidable estate, he conveyed certain mixed feelings about his life, but was very clear about his goals:

"I should not be happy because I am staying in such a luxurious house. Ultimately, my goal should be—and my goal is (but I don't know how soon I will achieve it)—to become...to give up all this...to be so simple, so that I only think about my soul and nothing else, and do the minimum of killing... Our monks walk. I travel in a car, enjoy travelling in a car. Actually—ultimately—I should begin to walk on my own and see that I do not kill anything."

For the Jains, such so-called revelations are self-evident and have been put into practice to varying degrees for several thousand years. In an interview with the Dalai Lama, His Holiness made clear [22] that the Jains were enormously influential in conveying to the first Buddhists the true meaning of "love of life and respect for all sentient beings."

His Holiness went on to say, "Everybody, of course, you see, saying(sic) importance of peace, of world peace, peace everywhere. Politicians, religious persons, in many circles people use this word. But peace, you see, can not come from the sky, or come from the earth. Peace..." (he paused, weighing his words in that extraordinarily emotive, Tibetan-inflected certitude that lends such genuine vivacity to his way of speaking), "Since destruction (similarly) does not come from (the sky or the earth), from either side—destruction is by the human being—so equally, the opposite...genuine peace, lasting world peace, also must, you see, come from the human being, (from) oneself."

Indian scholars have pointed out passages in the Buddhist canons which strongly suggest that Buddha was a disciple of Parshva prior to his own enlightenment. Buddha is said to have stated,

"I lived nude, took my food in hands; and neither took food brought to me, nor aimed at and nor by invitation. I uprooted my hair, showed mercy even to a drop of water, lest any invisible animate being should be killed by me. For this, I remained minutely careful. Even in winter and summer I lived nude in a horrible forest, and never warmed my body; always meditating like a muni."[23]

Buddha did not advocate a life of asceticism, though many of his Theravada and Hinayana disciples preferred the more extreme ascetical approach. Buddha adopted the *Madhyama prati-pat*, or Middle Path, an expedient of least resistance. Mahavira, in the tradition of his Jina predecessors, like the Parshva upon whom Buddha evidently modelled his earliest ascetic retreat, sought a far more rigorous and absolute behavioral pattern that would guarantee a painless existence for every living creature. He was thus known, in Buddhist texts, as a *Nigantha*, literally, one who is free from all possessions. It must be remembered, however, that from the Jain perspective, there is nothing *extreme* about the path of liberation, the slow progress towards moksha. Moksha, final release, *is* absolute, and utterly incommensurate with ordinary life. To a Digambara monk who has relinquished everything, there is nothing extreme. Such a monk would find a jail cell in the Sahara as suitable as Rio during Mardi Gras or the Library of Congress, for the cultivation of his soul and the absolute control of his inner world.

This absolute approach to moksha which Jain moral behavior has adopted—however fraught with the normal inconsistencies of human nature (whose acknowledgment forms the rightful basis for any path upon which a people must struggle)—is reflected on many levels in daily Jain life. The fact, for example, that there is virtually no record of Jain crime in modern India; and that few Jains can be found in the military. While Jains provided sanctuary for both Hindus and Moslems during the turmoil following India's independence, the Jain community has always been essentially neutral, a window of conscience overlooking the surrounding world—a little Switzerland embedded in a turbulent and fast changing nation.

Their neutrality hinges, again, on the realization that interference, per se, is frequently untoward. But this does not mean that they don't forcefully disapprove of violence in any form. It is worth quoting from Chhogmal Choprha's work outlining the behavior and tenets of the Terapanthi:

"Jainism enjoins complete non-injury to sentient beings and the Jain Shvetambara Terapanthi sadhus strictly observe this Sastric injunction and preach the same to others. Even in scorching heat they do not use fans, as that causes injury to the air lives; even in shivering cold they do not warm themselves at a fire-side, as that injures fire lives; they do not touch green vegetables, plants, and grass etc., as that causes injury to the vegetable lives; they do not drink water from a river, pool, or well, as that is injuring the water lives. They drink boiled or inanimate water only and beg the same from householders. Their faith prohibits them from countenancing or supporting any act whereby any sentient being is hurt, injured or killed."[24]

This statement intones the strict behavioral code of monks. Modern lay Jains are less likely to avoid touching plants, to be sure. In the same way, obviously, wheat harvesting and the heavy manufacture of radiators is bound to kill organisms. Such differences between monks and lay votaries, or even assimilated Jains, find analogous contradiction in any world religion.

The Hasidim of the Mea Sharim in Jerusalem, for example, practice an Orthodox Judaism altogether foreign from that which the normal Reform Jew in France, or America, is likely to undertake. Yet both sects are oriented towards the same Judaic goals. The Hasidim are likely to commit their every waking moment to their faith, while the assimilated Jew may do so twice a year, at sobering holidays. Yet the assimilated Jew is unceasingly *about* Judaism, to the extent that he feels, knows, abides by the spirit of his ancestors and beliefs. This ethnic quality of mind, having been freed of earlier ghettoized centuries, has the luxury in most countries today, of being a tiny minority that does not dictate national policy, or have to confront many state and federal laws which might well conflict with Orthodox Judaism. In Israel, however, the Knesset—whose members include representatives of the Hasidim—is constantly embroiled over the issue of the Old Testament, versus what is practical in a modern state.

The Jains have always been an utter minority within a vast, sprawling country. They too have had the greater protection of a Brahmanical society whose various Hindu sects—and for several centuries, Arab rulers—were normally charged with developing national policy. This shelter of the masses has meant that the Jains have been able to pursue their private goals as a cohesive community, without having to confront—at least in a practical sense—some of the tough issues of foreign policy, or of a national agenda. In a sense, they have been spoiled. They have been able to pursue certain ends without being held accountable, at least by the great population of non-Jains.

On the other hand, the inner nature of Jain accountability is as severe and telling as any doctrine, religion or philosophy the world has ever known. That responsibility to the soul entails an active position in the world by logical associations more compelling than mere administrative policy or national consensus.

Jains are thus not passive. Non-violence should never be taken to mean that Jains will not protect their homeland, or their loved ones. We reach a fine line here that ultimately, say the Jains, steps forward to defend its principles. Jains could not sanction a first strike, and no military hero can achieve salvation for his deeds. Nevertheless, self-defense, when necessary, defense of one's country and of loved ones as a last resort, is totally encouraged by Jainism. Only monks must never fight.

It is often said that non-violence is a lofty ideal in an imperfect world. But non-violence has indeed worked for the Jains. It could work for everyone. According to the principles of ahimsa that workability begins at home, around the dinner table, among friends, and at one's job. Carl Jung called this the 'heroism of everyday.' The hero of modern times is the individual who is aware of his or her actions and takes deliberate measures to ensure that his path is a harmless one. The outward trappings are not particularly striking, valiant, or famous. But they are enormously rewarding, and effective.

Preventing pain is difficult, and it is not difficult. What do I mean? For the Jains it is obvious. At a Jain school for children in Bombay, I witnessed a daily meditation among the kids, preceding their immersion into math, literature and history. The meditation was quite simple. The teacher merely asked them to concentrate on peace; to think of their favorite animals; and to figure out new and ingenious ways by which they could make those animals happy. The children were to silently concentrate on these heady issues for forty-eight minutes at the beginning of each day.

Jainism is revolutionary, persuasively capitalistic, incredibly successful. Its success is expressly a function of its gentleness. I would like to believe—indeed, I must hold out hope—that there is a little bit of the Jain in everybody. This is the beginning

The Genesis of Ahimsa

NOT ONE DAY HAS PASSED IN MY LIFE that I have not come upon the terrible, unendurable suffering of an animal, and suffered myself as a result, weighed down in my heart by the unimaginable forbearance of creatures that have had to contend with the human presence. We leave footprints the size of dinosaurs, fumbling, interrupting, inflicting harm wherever we tread. The damage which we commit, our throw-weight, far exceeds our abilities at restitution. In countless instances I have happened upon the remains of a deliberate action.

Once, for example, I saw a fisherman who was in the act of catching a small sting ray. He dragged it in, decided he didn't want it, ripped the inordinately large hook from the animal's insides, pulling a considerable portion of internal organs with it. The man tossed the fish to the side, where the poor critter writhed and cried out in agony. I called the man a bastard, raised my fists, and the passions swelled in my head until I became dizzy. The sting ray stared at me in his death throes. I lifted him, and placed him in the waves, where he sank to the bottom. Where I sank to the bottom.

In New York there was a mouse flattened atop a slab of concrete in the middle of that insensitive, teeming morass; its legs had been pulled off, its remaining body wracked with doom and left for the ants. In the Greek highlands I discovered an old mule tied to a stake, its body tangled in barbed wire, starved, without water, begging to die. I once found an abandoned puppy placed on a cliff ledge along a river in Tennessee. It had been cast off by a hillbilly, had not had food or drink for days; and a monkey near the Louvre, chained miserably to a music grinder's apparatus; caged fowl and a whole row of little puppies, considered tasty in Beijing, knowingly awaiting their coming slaughter; a beautiful Doberman shaking convulsively as attendants dragged it into the execution room, where an injection put it to sleep, like so many other millions of hapless cast-aways each year, all of whom know, peering out into the hazy labyrinth of human gigantism, with its seemingly gentle strokes and lulling words—"It's OK sweetheart"—that they will be systematically killed; a lost, bewildered coyote that had ventured into traffic one night on the Los Angeles freeway, disappearing beneath the unstoppable onrush. I still hear the howls, as they were muffled, bounced, silenced. It is a pain that lingers long after the death of an innocent animal. A pain that shouldn't be there. We all have our own horror stories. Life has inundated us with them.

I know of no greater relief—call it pleasure, momentary salvation, the gripping discovery of vulnerability all around us, with nobody in control; no finer sobriety than the rescue of another being, the exertion of the megatonnage in our conscience. Just this morning, I plucked a mosquito from a bowl of our parrot Stanley's drinking water. The mosquito had been there a long time, perhaps all night. I thought she was dead. Ever so gently I removed her to my fingertip, whence suddenly her delicately painted body began to quake, her wings fumbled, her head looked up. If I'd had the proper recording equipment, I might have heard her heart pumping furiously, her lungs gasping, and that still small voice crying out. I set this little girl of a mosquito down upon a leaf.

And reflecting on that little kid—as I prefer to remember all of them—I imagine myself on the moon, marooned, bereft of all life and condemned to staring nostalgically down at the earth. Among those barren lunar dunes and futile hillocks, a single mosquito's comradeship, with its commonality of purpose—to live—would be a divine deliverance. Someone to talk to. Someone to hold on my fingertip and whisper sweet nothings to. Short of that mosquito—whose biochemistry, behavior, brain and soul can not be re-created at any price—the moon would be an empty nightmare.

This isn't to say that I don't personally agree with the humorist who noted, 'Those who deny that little things in life can be monstrous annoyances have never spent an un-airconditioned summer night cooped up in a lousy motel room with one, loud mosquito.'

If life and death were simply biological, perfectly physical, cyclical, ecological, leaves making humus, humus re-making leaves, there would be no such aftermath of bereavement, with respect to the visitation of injury and pain on all life forms. I can only explain the bitter and intolerable feelings that accompany the experience of another animal's cry in the dark as coming from some immaterial place of primacy. I assume that place must be the soul. It is vulnerable, and no amount of beauty—or annoyance—seems capable of assuaging it. For the Jain, ever mindful of moksha, final release comes when one has made peace with such pain.

How does one even begin to make peace with it? The realization of such frailty and pain as exist in our world, has prompted most of Jainism. One outstanding example of the path to liberation is that of the twenty-second Tirthankara Arishtanemi (or Neminatha as he is called). It is said that he was on his way to be married to the beautiful Rajamati in the house of his future father-in-law when he heard the cries of some animals that were tied down. Upon inquiry, he learned that these creatures were to be killed in order to feed the guests at his own wedding. Instantly his "heart melted," he forswore his marriage and embarked on a life of asceticism in the mountains. Rajamati joined him and the two renunciates lived as mendicants. After a lifetime of preaching compassion and self-control, Neminatha achieved enlightenment at the cliff sanctuary of Girnar. Upon his death, he was liberated.

The twenty-third Tirthankara, Parshvanatha (Parshva), came to a similar vantage point on the universality of suffering when he encountered an ascetic in the forest (his own maternal grandfather) whose carelessness resulted in the death of two innocent snakes. The outcome of this experience was to induce Parshvanatha to seek to remedy pain forevermore according to the three jewels—Right Faith, Knowledge, and Conduct—and the principles of *samayika* (introspection), and *samyama* (self-restraint). This humane defiance of laziness, ineptitude, willful, even unconscious destruction; this delicate scaffolding of behavioral controls and affirmations is the beginning of reconciliation with pain.[25]

Such suffering is universal. All life forms suffer some of the time, or all of the time; and still others suffer on their behalf. If we had the world to make over again, surely we would eliminate suffering, and all of the pain and cruelty that are so everywhere inherent, it seems, to evolution, to the mingling of species, and the relations of people. All animals kill, either through their seemingly harmless nibbling upon plants, or their more zealous predation upon other animals (heterotrophy). In the case of we humans, several hundred million of us have been murdered over the years by other humans. Even during the height of the Renaissance, for all of its artistry, gentle moderation, insight and humanism, some seven million people were massacred, and not a few cannabilized, as the result of various religious wars and persecutions.

This condition of resulting anguish has engendered a rich futility of despair. I recall the many "carnal, bloody and unnatural acts" throughout Shakespeare and so much of German and Italian opera. Hemingway's haunting description of the Spanish Civil War for *Pravda* echos like a tenaciously true whisper in my gut:

"You see the murdered children with their twisted legs, their arms that bend in wrong directions, and their plaster powdered faces. You see the women, sometimes unmarked when they die from concussion, their faces grey, green matter running out of

their mouths from bursted gall bladders... You see them sometimes blown capriciously into fragments as an insane butcher
might sever a carcass..."[26]

— And I think of Francis Bacon's agonized *Baboon Study*, the
creature shadowed, condemned behind wire, reaching for impos-
sible rescue, or Francisco Goya's wrenching firing squad in his
Third of May, 1808. We have not ignored our self-abuse. Picasso's
Guernica, Jaroslav Hasek's *The Good Soldier Schweik*, Charlie Chap-
lin's *Soldier Arms*, Brecht's *Mother Courage*, E. M. Remarque's *All
Quiet on the Western Front*, Mailer's *Naked and the Dead*, or nine-
teenth-century photographer Felice Beatto's nauseating *Execution
Ground*, depicting a crucifixion and several skewered heads in
Meiji Japan, have each addressed a hideous region of insanity and
pleaded with an audience. More recently still, films like *Apocalypse
Now*, or *Ran* have surely driven home the aesthetic of marauding
vengeance, our fascination with horror, and the artistic rumina-
tions that can result. Television has of course served this fascination. We have all witnessed the clubbing of harp seals, the sickening slaughter of bison and whales, the remains of napalmed
Vietnamese or gunned-down L.A. gang victims (twelve in one
weekend in late 1990). And we watched the first night the allied
coalition bombed Baghdad like excited pyromaniacs.

Yet few of us have wandered through a slaughter house, I
imagine. I did it one night in a small town, while the young
employees were sharpening their knifes, which is how they did
the sheep in. It was a dimly lit warehouse with a blood-splattered
concrete floor. Hooks and chains hung here and there, bits of
flesh, bone, and an occasional eyeball lay withered and splayed in
corner heaps. I'll never be able to exorcise that galling sight, any
more than I will forget time spent in a refugee camp outside of
Dacca, where thousands of Bengalis had been placed. They were
starving to death and there was insufficient powdered milk and
biscuits to go around. Whatever international largesse had been
extended to Bangladesh, these people were the forgotten losers,
dying in anonymous clusters of human disaster. There was no
hope and they seemed to know it.

The romance of violence is the most successful Hollywood formula in the world today. When Edmund Burke defined the "sublime," he did so by relying on the premise that "pain can be a cause of delight," and that terror, danger, blackness, and the most violent disorders, are—in their effect on the mind—not unlike the sublime passions.[27] If one describes *Guernica* as beautiful or sublime, then Burke's understanding of the peculiar link between pain and pleasure surfaces, however unsettling and false that connection. Its semantic hyperbole assumes greater proportions when we recall that Picasso had stated in the late 1940s, "Art is the sum total of destruction."

But it is equally true that most people have little patience, and less of a stomach, for (real) horror stories, whether of animal abuse or the Holocaust. Their personal sensitivity seems destined to heal only by the opiate of disassociation, or the power of positive thinking. Others have denied the existence of such pain, reducing the world's daily agony to the mere "banality of evil," as Hannah Arendt termed it; the commonplace. Horror is easier to handle, that way. Certainly the perception of the "villain" motivates every consensus, from box office receipts to a U.N. security council resolution. But there is never any retribution for the innocent, no consensus on reparations other than a trifling dollar figure, or national apology, or bronze memorial.

And it is no wonder: our lives move past us with the alacrity of a tropical storm. By morning no one remembers who we were. Animals pass through this life with even greater speed, though the owl and the parrot, the loon and the white sturgeon, the whale and the wolf, live long lives (two hundred years or more for a sturgeon), and have genetic memories exceeding one hundred million years. Nevertheless, we treat them as ephemera; we treat ourselves that way. The only consolation is our fragile art which tries to linger, and the haphazard, private pleasures which come from connecting with another species.

Our lives are tailored towards curbing the realization of the finite. We inflate experience, blindly seeking an anaesthetic that persuades or tricks an otherwise intolerable pain into thinking happy thoughts, instead. This is how most people turn their backs on the reality of where their fancy-wrapped chicken breasts in lemon sauce come from.

I managed to save the Greek mule and the Tennessee puppy, for a time. But nothing I could do was going to ease the agony of that sting ray, that mouse, that coyote, or the Doberman. Or all the other fated little kids that beg for mercy, that wonder why? inside me. Like an icon of lingering, unimaginable endurance, the innocent afflict me in the mind-driven aftermath. Stricken conscience, coated in oil, tormented by so many vivisections of my own species, to which I, like it or not, belong.

Given this infuriating paralysis, it is no wonder that our art, our love affairs, and idealisms are turned, predominantly, away from an unnegotiable world of tooth and claw, of eat and be eaten, and oriented instead towards a more realizable goal of happiness. Because in the end, how does one fight it? Aristotle called this inevitability-charged plateau, the all-knowing surrender which Buddhism commends, as the *summum bonum*, or natural end of all human beings.

Our ability to dwell upon beauty suggests a crucial corollary to pain, which is the moral core of art. Morality cannot dictate art, nor art morality. Yet the two are linked, just as thought and deed are forever testing the possibilities of their inextricability. The collective affirmation that is the vast majority of our art, is rather inseparable from a moral stance. Affirmation conveys hope. Hope, in turn, yearns after substance which is higher, more singular and long-lasting than the desire for mere gratification. That substance is delicate, alive, radical. One need not surrender. And Jainism is my witness.

In spite of the habitual fall into violence that marks our schizoid other, this intangible flame has not gone out. It is the soul of art. It is certainly part of the soul. We hope not only for its well-being, but its immortality. And such affirmation, in the face of our mortality, on whatever level, strikes of a certain possibility—in life as in death—that is generous and inherent and beautiful.

The great work of art invariably takes a position, knowing or unknowing. It fosters that substance, and in so doing, affirms the possibilities of the soul, what the ancient Greeks called *synderesis*, spark of conscience. The Egyptians knew it to be the *ba*. The process of such affirmation categorically rejecting brutality, I would venture, is nature acting out impulses that have become self-aware. We have given to nature this option, in ourselves. Because of its uniquely affirmative goal, beyond the contradictions which it has struggled to surmount, it is nature, but it is also something other than nature. It holds in its mind an idea that transcends the unfairness of evolution and mere survival, of which it is of course a by-product.

This perception of nature is inventive, and imagines a world composed of the same beauties and miracles, but lacking the aggression. In effect, it conceives of a slightly different mechanism whereby, proverbially, the lion and the lamb whisper love mutterings to one another. And why not? The inane suggestion that the world simply doesn't behave that way is insufficient to arrest other powers of positive thinking; powers capable of transformation, of effecting new schemes.

The domestication of the wild dog was one such scheme. All of agriculture stems from this *taming* instinct in man. And without belaboring the verb, to tame, to nurture, foster and engender, are the very techniques of love, understanding, art. To mollify for purposes of friendship, to affirm, again, a relationship of joy where fear and danger existed previously, as in the case of the wild dog, is the spiritual in man. And it is all about us.

Against the presence of such soul, humanity's shortcomings are all the more perplexing. What prevents us from inhabiting that transcendental moment, always? The paradise factor in the human psyche is accustomed to collisions and grueling marathons. We continue to inflict pain and each of us knows this aspect of our genetic inheritance to be a fact of life. Human contradictions are daunting. They lend themselves to all those philosophies of good and evil; to damnable Crusades and glaring symbolism, sobering hindsight, and the fall from every innocence. But they also lend themselves to Sistine Chapels, and to Jainism.

The desert monks of early Christianity had renounced violence by renouncing the world. Tibetan ascetics found their paradise closer to home, in the remote caves and mountains of the Himalayan outback. Chinese painters and poets reduced the scope of that yearning to the subtler dimensions of a hanging silk scroll, or obscure figure of speech, while Japanese savants cultivated that same so called *Pure Land* in the confined infinity of a tea house or sand garden, even in the palm of one's hand. In each instance, the evolution of an ideal came about through analogy that enabled us to reduce the impact of our perjorative psyche, and emphasize our positive one. In this manner, our original, untainted nature was obtainable in the landscape. Nature had become a stage on which a dramatic narcissism threw off the yoke of tyranny and re-claimed title to its earliest fantasies, with the added experience of an harmonious introspection.

Implicit in this self-interest was a genuine perception of beauty, and the spiritual finesse, the very tools, with which to fashion some of the grandest spectacles ever envisioned. Aside from the occasional distinguished Shogun, or celebrated disciple, we will never know the many other thousands of fellow artists, monks and patrons who sat staring at the work of art, or whispering to themselves the many mantras and philosophical treatises of their faith—hypnotized. These were the unsung beneficiaries of a monumental purpose, namely, the engendering of harmony on earth.

In Jainist India that original nature, that soul, did everything in its power to avoid the hypnotic, to transform that yoke into a different kind of endeavor, namely, the absolute exercise of restraint. But it was no less a masterful art form. Indeed, I perceive Jainism to be perhaps the most subtle and important art form—a living art form—ever conceived by any collective.

Among the Jains, soul (jiva) and life are synonymous terms. You can not have one without the other, and thus the perception of life, the vision of nature for the Jains, has always been tantamount to inner feeling, or self-awareness. Violence towards others is automatically understood as violence towards one self. Given the pain which is everywhere manifested in the world; the contra-

dictory nature of the sublime, and the fickleness of human behavior, Jainism has formulated a way of life, and a practical approach
to nature which is unapologetically severe. Its self-control is
intended to 'fence in' the otherwise unrestrainable passions that
can act for better or for worse. Knowing the proclivity for violence
which is in our clumsiness, in the unpredictability of our free-will
and our moods, and thus, by Jain inference, in the nature of the
world; and appreciating the aversion to pain which all organisms
share, the Jains have emphasized non-violence as the very core of
what is arguably the oldest living religion in the world.

The Jains have relentlessly undertaken to tame the wild dog
in each of us, not from any hedonistic yearning for power, or
selfish pleasure, but in order to reduce suffering and enhance the
general well-being. And they have done so in a manner similar to a
painter who wanders out into a meadow with oils and easel and
there faithfully reproduces nature, while adding a human touch,
the touch of non-violence. Jains accomplish this work of art, this
perception of nature, according to an explicit philosophy of absolute non-interference. The painter does not put down his brush,
walk over to the tree and bend down its branches—like the bonsai
horticulturalist—in order to better suit them to the composition
he may have in mind. The Jain composition will emphasize the
bending of the painter's own mental branches, not the tree's.
These dual impulses to tame, whilst not interfering, are not at all
incompatible, once the artist has seen through what the Jains term
darsana-mohaniya, the vast labyrinth of worldly *karmas* or *karman*
which impede the soul's self-knowledge and nature. Karma has
been broken down into its incremental injuriousness. For example, the Jains have identified which types of karma are notorious
for obscuring the jiva's perceptual, and epistemological capabili-
ties; and which karmas impede the soul's capacity for infinite bliss
and infinite power. [28]

There are eight paramount karman, pertaining to knowledge,
intuition, and feeling; to the source of all delusions, the determi-
nation of life-spans, of body, and of rank; and to karman which
generically is at the root of all hindrances in life.[29] Those impediments or physical fetters constrain the incarnate soul between the

siddha, or liberated, and the *samsari*, or mundane. Within that vast range of experience is every transgression, hope, pleasure, pain and breakthrough.[30]

Indeed, the oldest extant Jain canonical work, the *Acaranga Sutra*, makes it quite clear that the so-called contradiction alluded to above—that of artistic passivity versus active non-violence—is no contradiction:

"...a wise man should not act sinfully towards animals, nor cause others to act so, nor allow others to act so." [31]

This latter exhortation—*nor allow others to act so*—simply stated, opens up whole worlds of decisive, non-violent action. What constitutes the successful prosecution of an ideal has been much discussed in Jainism. We have already seen such active intercessions as the Jain animal sanctuaries. Yet given its doctrinal propensity to remain neutral, to neither exhibit nor interfere, the Jains might well have boxed themselves into a double-bind of schizophrenic magnitudes and frustratingly ineffective theory. But this has not been the case at all. They have thoroughly anticipated—indeed discovered through analysis—the many contradictions inherent to non-violence and their earliest canonical books, the *Angas*, copiously explore the options open to one who would refrain from harming any other organism on earth.[32]

There are twelve such Angas (limbs):

1) *Acara*, treating of the life of Mahavira and the rules of behavior for a monk.

2) *Sutrakrta*, which purports to clarify and counter prevailing heresies (we're speaking long before the time of Christ).

3) *Sthana* (cases), an encylopedic treatise on Jain doctrines presented in a numerically aggregated fashion, beginning with one and concluding with ten, so as to render it more accessible to readers.

4) The *Samavaya*, which continues the wide-ranging discourses of the third Anga, while intoning the fullest summary of all the Angas combined..

5) The *Vyakhyaprajnapti*, also known as *Bhagavati*. Forty-one parts treating of an enormous canvas—philosophy, ethics, mathematics, the theory of knowledge, cosmology. Much of it was written in the form of questions and answers between Mahavira and his disciple, Indrabhuti Gautama.

6) *Jnatadharmakatha*, pertaining to questions of morality, and written essentially for non-monks.

7) The *Upasakada* treats of lay-votaries and their observances.

8) *Antakrddasa* is devoted to the explication of liberated souls. It traces the *tapas* or austerities undertaken by various ascetics.

9) *Anuttaraupapatikadasa* treats of specific instances of reincarnation.

10) The *Prasnavyakarana* is focused, literally, on the perilous itineraries of karma.

11) The *Vipakasruta* analyses causality with respect to the outcome of our actions, both good and bad.

12) The *Drstivada* manuscript has been lost.

The Angas are only the beginning. Jain literary output is unprecedented. Like the Jews, Jains are people of the book. The 34 *Angabahyas*, 12 *Upangas*, 4 *Mulasutras*, 6 *Chedasutras*, 2 *Culikasutras*, and 10 *Prakirnakas*, all written in the Magadhan vernacular of Ardha-Magadhi, escalate the levels of analysis, of history, anecdote, the sciences, monastic rules, postures and penances, grammar and logic, metaphysics and diet, medicine, embryology, behavior at death, astrology, ontology, philosophy, law, and ethics. And all are uniformly addressed to the underlying assertiveness of Jain non-violence.[33]

Throughout the early Jain texts, one finds an emphasis, in fact, upon "willed action,"*(Kriya)*.[34] The basis for this willpower is the soul. All of its endeavors to expunge unwanted attachments, and to remediate agony all around it, stem from that imperceptible atomic presence, the cornerstone of what it is to be a human being nurturing a soul, jiva, the life force. To the extent that life is perpetually swept over by contradictions, so too the student of Jainism is caught up in dualistic affiliations. On the one hand are the decrees for action which Kriya—and a Gandhi—convey. At the same time are the varied and profound insinuations of a deep passivity that has resulted in a religion of easily perceived withdrawal.

But any such contradictions are quickly erased upon stepping into the real world of Jainism, where withdrawal is merely the *weather*, the deceptive cloud-cover concealing radical reform, trenchant and assiduous thought, unstinting compassion.

Ahimsa has always been known as the appreciable god of Jainism, its religion. For the great sage Amritacandra Suri, ahimsa's deeper associations pertained to lack of attachment and lack of passion. For Hemachandra, ahimsa was "the beneficient mother of all beings." As cited in Dr. L. M. Singhvi's essay *Jain Declaration On Nature*, (presented to His Royal Highness Prince Philip in October of 1990 at Buckingham Palace) the Jain scriptures read,

"All the Arhats (Venerable Ones) of the past, present and future discourse, counsel, proclaim, propound and prescribe thus in unison: Do not injure, abuse, oppress, enslave, insult, torment, torture or kill any creature or living being."

For Samantabhadra, ahimsa was "the highest bliss."[35] This was the ultimate essence of ahimsa, despite a Jain theology that claims no attachment to pain or pleasure, to passion or interest of any kind. One might argue that the poetic soul of Samantabhara was here speaking. Indeed, Jain prose and poetry is frequently lush, intoxicating; poetry in the greatest sense of the word. Call it contradictory, call it human—it is all part of Jainism.

Seated in a meadow beneath the burning, afternoon sun atop Mt. Abu, Professor Padmanabh S. Jaini of the University of California-Berkeley, spoke to me informally of ahimsa:

"As someone who was brought up as a Jain, I might say that what impresses me most about this religion is its unconditional respect for all forms of life. The Jains believe that each and every individual, however small, is capable of attaining salvation and must be allowed to do so in its own manner and must not be interfered with by our careless behavior. And that is for him the true gist of ahimsa: not to hurt oneself, and not to hurt any other beings."

For the common man, ahimsa was broken down according to the mental intention to cause pain (*bhava-himsa*) and the actual enactment of pain (*dravya-himsa*). The purpose of this delineation served the psychoanalysis which, to a casual observer, appeared obsessive but was in fact elementary. The Jains have enumerated with gusto those common pitfalls of behavior which so perversely lend themselves to the deliberate or inadvertent infliction of pain. And in every case, a little forethought can go a long way towards eradicating harm and nourishing conviviality.

For the householder, six general categories of occupation have always been deemed permissible, in spite of their known tendency to cause pain. Those job-types include military service, even handling of a weapon; production of consumer goods; cultivation of the arts; the use of ink; agriculture and construction. Within these *himsa* (harm)-incurring activities, however, there are hundreds of restraints stipulated. No deliberate injury, passion, falsehood is vouchsafed; nor the keeping of pets, or servants, or tied-down prisoners; no support of circuses; no bullock carts; no animal products; no stripping of bark or cutting down of trees; no use of weapons offensively, and so on.

There are actually fifteen occupations which are considered "cruel," and are absolutely forbidden. They are a livelihood involving charcoal, wood, carts, transport fees, hewing, animal by-products, insect secretions (shellac), alcohol, trade in human beings or animals, poisonous articles (thus nearly every chemical or agricultural product, and consequently all derivative professions using chemicals), activities that involve milling, mutilation, fire, the draining of swamps or lakes or the diverting of rivers, and a livelihood deriving from the propagation of anti-social behavior.[36] From the above, it is clear that within the lay Jain occupational world, whether in ancient times, or today, there are bound to be innumerable collisions of doctrine and practice.

The restrictions mount up rapidly to the point where—for the religious Jain—it becomes too much trouble to attempt any profession that has the slightest possibility of injury. Yet the practical nature of Jainism reveals itself. Professions are not altogether barred to a young person getting started in life. There are numerous options. And indeed, as has been described, the Jains have become enormously wealthy. Taking three non-violent steps backward for every slightly aggressive step forward, Jain civilization has achieved what is normally called progress without making a mess of its environment or particularly harming other beings. And this sociological lesson is the achievement, primarily, of ordinary people motivated, in large measure, by their monks who have made the ultimate sacrifices.

For the secular world of Jainism, there is no latitude out in the world. A monk's vows commit him, or her, to becoming a beacon of purity. Beacons generally evoke raised brows in the twentieth century. The unbridled, often out-of-tune dogma of ecclesiastics, and the contradictory lessons of theological history have given us sufficient cause to doubt the veracity or staying power of outmoded, often tyrannical conventions.

But Jain monks, in being largely without church, prospects for administrative power, or personal gain, are—in the purest, most abject sense of the phrase—possessionless, living from day to day, totally mindful of their responsibilities to life, constantly in the public eye and vulnerable to the censure of an orthodox expectation from which they never deviate.

Looking into the monks' eyes carried the intensity of an animal's inquisitive, loving stare—the best of us distilled into a glance; life tenderly gazing upon itself. Thus, the extraordinary challenge: to re-focus; to re-shape one's heart; to be kind and true and live deliberately.

CHAPTER FOUR

A Morning With the Digambara

THE TWO JAIN TEMPLES OF TARANGA sit on a high, dry Gujarati plain surrounded by granitic hillocks. Constructed in the characteristic fashion of white marble, their exteriors elaborately sculpted to reflect the Jain pantheon of sages, disciples, and associated animals, particularly the elephant, they were built in the thirteenth century, and refurbished three hundred years later. Dozens of white graceful monkeys inhabit the tiny village of Taranga, scampering along the walls surrounding the religious edifice, crowding the scant forest. The night before I had arrived, a tiger had been seen up among the large boulders on the adjoining slopes.

It was a bright cool December morning. I sat waiting before the entrance to a large cave behind the temples. Within a few minutes, two naked Digambara (sky-clad) monks emerged. One of them was in his forties, the other probably in his late sixties. In their hands they carried their two sole possessions in life, a *pinchi* (broom of peacock feathers), and a *kamandalu* (a gourd) for boiled water. We exchanged greetings and spent the morning together.

While there are over five thousand Jain monks and nuns, there are only some sixty-five Digambara ascetics left in India. Their nudity is a sacred trust, the ultimate form of renunciation and purity. But there is much more to be said for it than that. Their nudity cuts through the aforementioned contradictions in human behavior, reflecting an inner goal of self-control which they and their former teachers have pursued since Jainism began, many thousands of years ago.

One of Alexander the Great's biographers is alleged to have stated, in a now lost history, that the impetuous young Alexander abandoned all future conquests across Asia when, in 325 B.C., he encountered several such naked men sitting quietly in the Indian village of Taxila that lay directly in the path of his army. The ascetics would apparently not speak with Alexander until the young monarch took off his armour, sat down in the dust, and quieted his heart. It was thus that Alexander was humbled, and headed back home for Greece. I like the story, whether it's actually true or not, because it so patently expresses the inner logic motivating Digambara nudity, this total non-attachment, and unselfconscious quality of love which is their ahimsa. To say: here I am, this is all of me. I hide nothing, I have no shame, no regrets, nothing by me is concealed. You see the whole story, the whole me. There may not be the earth-jolting pronouncements of a Gorbachev, but such nudity—in its extraordinary honesty—stores up thousands of years-worth of truth and directness. We are all naked.

This issue of nudity (*acelakka*) was the preeminent source of disunity among Jains, a finite detail, perhaps, to outsiders, and one that is totally subsumed by the greater unity of ahimsa characterizing Jain devotion, regardless of sect. In actual fact, there are some eighteen points of difference between Shvetambaras and Digambaras, though none of these disparities encroach upon the core concepts of the Three Truths, the major vows, or the underlying assertion of ahimsa. Nevertheless, Shvetambara monks never go naked. The most advanced Digambara monks do so always. There was, it should be pointed out, an ancient compromise sect, the *Yapaniya*, who adopted nudity for monks, but also retained many of the Shvetambara scriptures. It is noteworthy, however, that both the first and the last tirthankaras adhered to the *Jinakalpa*, or nude mode of behavior, while the other twenty two tirthankaras were mixed on this issue.[37]

For the Digambara monk, the wearing of any clothing suggests "residual shame and thus negates all pretensions to monkhood." Whereas Shvetambara monks hold that while Mahavira was not in any way "attached" to his single garment, when he finally did dispatch with it, it was not because he felt nudity to be an essential component of the path to liberation.[38] Oddly, Digambaras and Shvetambaras have never resolved this difference. (To place it in a different context, it is interesting to remember that St. Francis, like St. John, also renounced all of his clothing, but only temporarily.)

The two monks proceed into the village, looking no more than six feet in front of them, gently brushing the path with their pinchis whenever possible so as to remove any insects likely to be in the way. They have already meditated on dozens of specific arenas of concern, gone out into the field for their toilet, avoiding twenty-two prohibited areas for 'easing nature,' swept the ground free of the last possible insect or germ, so as not to kill it with the weight of their falling feces, had a little boiled water to drink, and now venture towards this village to beg for their one meal of the day. The younger ascetic raises his hand to indicate his readiness to accept food. They will never take food for themselves, or touch a living thing. Without the complicity of disciples and lay followers, the ascetics will die, voluntarily starving to death.

Jain monks are devoted to achieving non-violence for all living beings. Their work is cut out for them and they know it. They spend their time largely in the company of people, or near enough to people to obtain their one meal of the day. An extraordinary relationship persists between mendicant and lay householder. To feed a Jain ascetic is an honor, dating back at least three thousand years.

As they approach a particular residence, where a family stands out front on the dirt walkway awaiting them, other local residents, children and adults alike, bow down before the faintly smiling ascetics. Once they have stepped up to the impoverished abode, three food-giving family members circle the ascetics reciting 'The Three Purities,' namely, that "this food is pure, my heart is pure, and what I am saying is true." The three family members have prepared the food in advance, according to a veritable science of non-violent botany prescribed by Jainism.

The old monk is fasting this day. He stays outside while the younger one enters the family's two-room abode. I follow him. He will eat standing upright. His hands are his begging bowl. The three people pour a thick lentil gruel into the monk's hands. He eats it slowly. They give him a nut. He sniffs it and lets it fall to the floor. For some reason it doesn't appeal to him. That particular nut might have violated one of several hundred rules for determining what kinds of food are allowed.

I would later discover that lay Jains have a fantastic culinary aptitude which is not curtailed in any significant way by their religious beliefs. And while they are lacto-vegetarians, they are not absolute vegetarians. They do not believe—at least in India—that dairy products inflict harm on the goats or cows or water buffalos (this latter animal providing milk of the highest concentration of protein). In countries like the United States where large-scale dairy farms are scandalous, the treatment of the animals abominable, it is unthinkable that the Jains would sanction such food.

Lay Jains fashion sumptuous meals from clarified butter, wheat flour breads like nan and rotli and chapati, spinach, soy, cabbage and pilau, plain boiled rice and lentils, fresh buttermilk, ground nuts, chilies, cinnamon, peppers and papaya, mangos and oranges, for a starter. On the other hand, one could find hundreds of foods that are off-limits to Jains.

The monks have an even narrower range of food to choose from, and it must be acknowledged that they are not thrilled about eating anything! They do so having insured the minimum of violence, and with the understanding that organisms on earth possess from one to five senses. Monks are restricted to certain types of one-sensed plants. The lay Jains are afforded a far wider latitude, but are nonetheless restricted to one-sensed plant food.

I watch the ascetic consume his meal, his eyes closed. When he was a young man one of his teachers, the spiritual leader, or acarya, of all Digambara monks, after decades of ascetic wandering, fasted to death whilst reciting the Jain prayers. His name was Santisagara (Ocean of peace) and it was September, 1955. From the year 1920, Santisagara had owned not a single possession, not even a loincloth.[39] His death was undertaken according to the prescriptions of the twenty-fourth, and most recent, Tirthankara or sage, Mahavira.

Both Mahavira and Buddha had similar lives, though Mahavira spent his entire career practising all of the self-restraints basic to Jainism, whereas Buddha spent but six years doing so, and—as mentioned earlier—did not subsequently avow such ascetic rites as particularly constructive. Both men renounced family and possessions and embarked on a road that would lead them towards peaceful immortality. Mahavira did so only after his parents had died, so as not to break their hearts. For the rest of his life he underwent every calamity and penance, cultivating the severest self-purification, single-mindedly pursuing the goal of *kaivalya*, or complete, undifferentiated consciousness, the forerunner of liberation.

Under an ashoka tree he plucked out his own hair in five clumps and became one of millions of homeless people. For thirteen months he wandered around in the clothes on his back, then discarded them, remaining naked for the rest of his life. The Digambaras and Shvetambaras debate over whether Mahavira had been married prior to his renunciation, the former sect alleging absolutely not, the latter, white-robed disciples arguing unanimously, yes. Mahavira delivered his first sermon atop a hill known as Vipulacala, not far from the town of Rajagrha. He spoke in the vernacular, thus forsaking the inaccessible Sanskrit of the pundits. In this manner, for thirty years, walking all over India, discussing his views, seeking solutions to the pain which he witnessed everywhere he travelled, Mahavira effected a spiritual revolution for the common man. Not unlike a Homer, or a Dante or a Shakespeare, Mahavira's inescapable *artistry* touched off an unquenchable thirst for emotional satisfaction in Indian culture which his eleven disciples or so called *ganadharas* (Indrabhuti Gautama and Sudharman foremost among them) would carry forth. From Sudharman to Jambu; from Jambu to Prabhava, to Shayyambhava and so on. When Mahavira died, he had nearly half-a-million Jain disciples.

Today there are between six-and-ten-million Jains (estimates vary). The more numerous Shvetambara include the sub-sects of the *Murtipujaka*, the *Sthanakavasi*, and the *Terapanthi*. The other major sect, Digambara, is divided into the *Bisapanthi*, *Terahapanthi*, and *Taranapanthi*. Their differences, at least to an outsider trying to obtain a mere foothold in this elusive religion, are seemingly minor. What is remarkable is their unanimity.

During Mahavira's time, there were by his own accounts 363 Jain schools of philosophy in India, the most prominent being those of the *Kriyavada*, a doctrine of *jiva*, or the soul. According to this creed, the soul was embodied (*bandha*) in *ajiva*, or non-soul, in other words, the body.[40] Through pious deeds and ceaseless concentration, one struggled to stave off the stampede of *karma*, harmful matter, and thus liberate the incarcerated soul in this life time. Mahavira himself accomplished this final breakthrough, or *moksha*, while meditating beneath a sala tree at Pava-puri in Bihar State, prior to passing away. The year was 527 B.C.. Totally tranquil, he was 72 years old at the time.[41] That spot, surrounded by five, palm-laden hills, is today a place of pilgrimage up through the month of March each year. A temple sits in a pool of lotuses. Inside the temple, Mahavira's footprints are to be found.

What altogether distinguished Mahavira's insights from those of later Buddhism and Hinduism was his emphasis on the *reality* of this world. He never postulated the oppressive maya, or illusion, that has provided a way out of emotional dilemmas for most other spiritual traditions. In promulgating a philosophy of the transient, by which all effort was deemed vain, all worldly accomplishment without substance, all goals delusory, Buddha succeeded in devaluing life and the miracle of earth in hopes of fostering a more solid appreciation for that intangible, eternal 'other', the nexus of nirvana. Nirvana has variously been defined as "extinction" and "total affirmation." Buddhism accomplishes this suspension of disbelief, this temptation towards nirvana, somewhere between death and reincarnation, through devout prayer and the guarantee of a bewildering pantheon of deities, many compassionate, none of them exactly of this earth.

Where Buddhism came magnificently to terms with life was in the importance it placed upon art, particularly in China and Japan, where paradise was conceived to exist within the confines of a certain garden or atop a sacred mountain, as replicated in a painting, or sculpture. Meditation on such paradise was conceived as a technique for launching the psyche into union with the source of its meditation, either through verbal recitation, or visualization.

Yet such artistic revery was limited in many ways, not only to the artist and his small coterie of admirers, but in the much greater exclusion of other animal species who were not able to partake of this aesthetic launching pad.

One can not overly emphasize the exquisite universality of Jainism. Mahavira bravely welcomed this earth, with its teeming obstacles and temptations. He understood that there was no 'other,' no promise of refuge, no escaping the blessed responsibility to all life with which we have been endowed, and with whom we are one.

Most crucially, Mahavira adopted what the Greeks would later term a *hylozoistic* approach to the natural world, a view that all matter contains soul; soul which is in a state of permanent, living, breathing, feeling flux. Thus, the clay-bound earth, water, the air, and fire—all are living organisms.[42] In one conversation between Mahavira and his disciple Gautama, the Jina is alleged to have stated that "the ultimate end of soul is samatva."[43] In other words, that the kernel of what makes a human being human, is the same kernel that makes every other organism itself. The kinship resulting from this psychological reciprocity is intrinsic to the life force, and to all ecology.

This basic biological urging has become introspective in homo sapiens; ecology—a reappraisal of self. The biosphere, all of the billions of organisms within its fold, are depending on our psychic avowal; our courtesy and etiquette; our moderation and our capacity for tears. We may well die without having learned any answers, but the same questions of a life force with which Jainism is pre-eminently concerned, will always prevail: questions concerning universal decency, and the possibilities of love.

Mahavira knew of twenty four types of beings, and five-hundred sixty-three body-types that partook of such reciprocity, in addition to nearly eight-hundred and seventy-five thousand different species identified by ancient Jain biologists. This scientific acumen was unmatched well into the twentieth century. For comparison, Aristotle, himself a biologist, knew of less than five hundred species.[44] And nowhere in Greek science or philosophy is the oneness of nature viewed as a psychic equality between all species. Plotinus (205-270 A.D.) in his *Enneads* came closest to postulating a biological similitude of cosmic proportions, namely, the *Nous*, or universal soul. But this figment of Plotinus's imagination had little or no bearing on the behavior, dignity, or integrity of human individuals here on earth.

Mahavira even went so far as to analyze soul clusters, such as coral, moss, algae, lichen, and posited the existence of the living equivalent of atoms, namely, nigodas. Jains knew of physical atoms long before the fifth century B.C. Greek philosopher Democritus described them. The Jains called them anu. Molecules were named skandha, and together they comprised the bases of all pudgala, or matter (ajiva). For every particle of matter, an urgent soul was interned, restive, fertile. That soul was capable of thought, bhava-samvara, a contemplative process given to shaking off the inrush of matter. These mentations and bio-dynamics engendered a host of unique associations symbolic of life and death, and oriented to a pensive river of self-awareness.

But the profound introversion was only as effective as its powers of observation. And this is especially important: it distinguishes the Jains from mere dreamers. Jains are all consummate biologists at heart. In the balance of interior dialogue and outer awareness lies an awesome embrace of life's cornucopia, understood by the Jains for the first time in all of its myriad complexity. While the Middle Kingdom Egyptians were building pyramids to house a few immortal Pharaohs, the Jains were building pyramids of thought to house an immortal earth with billions of immortal souls.

So profluent throughout the universe were these minutest of living creatures *(nigodas)* that they were to ensure a permanent stream of creation on earth. "This little 'I', which is the ever-agitated centre of our brief lives, is eternal," wrote Jagmanderlal Jaini, referring to the universal jiva.[45] Each nigoda had—has—an individual soul and destiny, infiltrating the soil, every root system, each plant, and fruit, and brain, and thus assisting in the cohesiveness of the biological impulse, with its prescribed evolutionary punctuation marks and gradations.

Jains know of thought-colors *(Leshya)*, thought-smells, of hierarchical tastes, and sights and sounds. All are prescribed with greater or lesser emphasis according to the weight of aversion or attraction deemed suitable in the ongoing struggle to extricate that marvelous spark of existence from the dark whorls of insensate substance.

The allegory associated with the leshyas provides insight into the behavioral delineations symptomatic of ahimsa. Six diverse individuals are said to approach a blackberry tree, each desiring to taste the fruit. He with the black hue fells the whole tree in order to eat one berry. The blue-hued individual severs the largest limb for the same purpose. The greyish-colored person cuts a smaller branch; the pale yellow man or woman extracts enormous clusters; the pink-traced being takes berries one by one; and finally, the white individual will take only those few berries which have already fallen to the ground.[46] The ecological nature of this moral is fundamental to Jainism. What has become known as "green party" environmentalism in the late twentieth century, was prescribed three thousand years ago by the followers of the Jinas.

According to this litany, souls bring upon themselves their next reincarnation according to the piety of their current life. A wholly pious nigoda today could well become a monk tomorrow, though not vice versa. The Jain monk thus serves as an evolutionary magnet.

Mahavira's village of Vaisali, modern Basarh, some twenty miles north of Patna on the Ganges, today pays tribute to its 2500 year old biological and spiritual legacy that was its most famous native son. Every year, Mahavira's nirvana is celebrated (not only in Basarh, but all over India) with the burning of candles. It is known as Diwali Day, a time of feasting, and it occurs early each winter.[47]

Jainism goes back in history several thousands of years, according to Jain belief. The first Tirthankara, or Jina, of our time was Rshabha. According to Jain legend, the country of India was named after his eldest son, Bharata. Rishabha is said to have been the first to preach ahimsa, before achieving his own kaivalya atop Mount Kailasha in the Himalayas (known to the Buddhists as Su-Meru, to the Tibetans as Dise). Documented evidence supports Jain geneological claims back at least to the early ninth century when the twenty-third Tirthankara, Parshva was born in Varanasi in 877 B.C., later achieving his supreme knowledge atop Mt. Sammedacala (Parasanatha Hill) in Bihar.[48] Nineteen other Tirthankaras achieved nirvana on this mountain. [49]

The enforced abolition of pain that was inherent to the ancient Niganthan creed, and to these twenty-four historical enlightenments, is outlined in the *Acaranga Sutra*. This was the first of twelve canonical angas purporting to reflect the teachings of Mahavira, memorized by disciples, but not committed to writing until the third or fourth century A.D., at which time the Shvetambara Jains gathered all of the existing documents together, and had monks speak aloud and transcribe everything that was purportedly remembered of the early religion.

"...all breathing, existing, living, sentient creatures should not be slain, nor treated with violence, nor abused, nor tormented, nor driven away. This is the pure, unchangeable, eternal law..." [50]

The Acaranga Sutra combines lyrical abstraction (which is symptomatic of the later pictorial traditions), with a host of trenchant observations into human nature. It is probably the first, and surely the most thorough psychoanalysis of violence ever set forth. And it is only the beginning of several hundred additional canonical works and commentaries treating of the subject in infinitessimal detail, not for the sake of scholarship, the pleasures of logical discourse, but in order to enshrine a viable lifestyle for monks and lay persons alike.

Many of the angas and subsequent commentaries relate their morals in the form of animal fable and philosophical anecdote, travelers's tales, adventure yarns, poetic effusions. One reads of horses trapped on far-off islands; efforts to purify polluted waters; the nineteenth Tirthankara Malli, a beautiful woman, exposing the banality of her body to would-be suitors; a frog who converts to Jainism; kidnappings, solitary suicides, a rash of enlightenments, endless renunciations.[51]

Animal spirituality is accorded particular emphasis, as could be expected.[52] Animals are abundantly depicted in the art, areas within temples are reserved for animals, and the many stories pertaining to the volitional, self-sacrificing acts of conscience by fish, cobras, horses, an elephant named Megha that dies as a result of saving a hare, and a lion in particular, all suggest important analogies with humankind. Animals can fast, take vows, renounce killing, and thereby achieve rebirth in heaven, or as human beings. That the animal spirit mingles in the same philosophical ether as that of the human means that one soul is equal to all souls, for the Jain. And this being so, to commit violence to one is to commit violence to oneself. This "Do Unto Others" maxim defines the fullest circle of the Jain transmigration of souls and conveys the supreme joy that can be gleaned through universal compassion.

What is particularly interesting about the sphere of *madhyaloka*, that cosmological quadrant reserved exclusively for animals and humans, is the Jain realization that violence in nature, be it human or animal-provoked, is wrong. Because there is no Jain god, creator of the universe, Jains have the religious freedom to chastise the workings of the world. Training one's dog not to bite, so to speak, Jains struggle to make evolution a safer, more benevolent system by which to live. It may well be the most important spiritual impulse that has ever been conceived: we are the architects of our destiny.

Unlike Buddhism, whose doctrinal emphasis lies with the monastic clergy, Jain commentators recognized that the monks, whose vows reflected the ultimate path, were nonetheless a small minority within Jain communities. It was deemed crucial that the average individual maintain an equally *attuned* (if less stringent) discipline. And so these scholars produced numerous texts known as *shravakacaras*, rules of behavior specifically for the layman.[53]

There are hundreds of such rules, though not the thousands which define the behavior of monks. The entire corpus is predicated upon the recognition of *himsa*, or violence, which exists all around us, and—even more importantly—inside us. Accordingly, there are external and internal austerities. *Avirati* (lack of control), has been intensively analyzed and broken down into five primary transgressions: injury, falsehood, stealing, incontinence and the desire for possessions.[54] This avirati applies to both thought and action. To commit a violent act is only slightly more offensive than to want to commit the act. Thus, the Acaranga Sutra states,

"That man (i.e. the liberated) conquers wrath, pride, deceit, and greed. This is the doctrine of the Seer who does not injure living beings...He who conquers one (passion) conquers many... Knowing the misery of the world...He who avoids one (passion), avoids (them all)..." [55]

Self-control is perceived as nothing more 'complicated' (can there be anything more difficult?) than the stopping of the influx of karma, a process known as *samvara*. The mental equipment necessary to effect the necessary restraint has been monumentally calculated according to twelve *anupreksha*s, or reflections. [56]

As I watch the Digambara monk finish his meal, after no more than a few minutes of eating time, and consider the fact that he has spent most of his life to-date, naked, sleeping on floors, rarely speaking, never eating after dark (insects could get in his food and he wouldn't see them), walking thousands of miles, it is tempting to compare him with the Milarepan prototype; that famed

Tibetan Buddhist mendicant, student of the great Sanskrit scholar Marpa, also naked, who had retired from the world to an icy cave in order to achieve, eventually, his personal nirvana. But such comparisons are utterly inappropriate.

Unlike Buddhism, or any other religion, Jain nirvana is expressly human-related, centered on earth, not in heaven. And while their cosmographical studies indicate specific heavens (in keeping with which, Jain astronomy and mathematics are alleged to have 'invented' the concept of infinity), such places are considered to be as detrimental to enlightenment as hell. Jains recognize karma, but unlike the Hindu or Buddhist, who conceive the physical universe as mere passing ephemera, the Jains believe it to be totally galvanizing, here and now, absolute, real. Nature is nature, in all of its exquisite diversity. But beauty has a price. The substratum of that nature, and of earth, is known as this karma, consisting of material atoms that flow into, and can (though need not) bind the soul, clouding its purity, and consequently condemning the organism to a life of lesser or greater violence.

What this really seems to mean is that while nature is perceived as beautiful, such wonders are not sufficient in and of themselves to curb the painful side of reality. Ecological Jainism is thus about stewardship, requiring human diligence, a human conscience.

Some karma—hereditary traits, for example—is considered normally harmless. Nor is karma seen as a basis for fatalism. Because of the incumbent choices that are fundamental to Jainism, human beings are spectacularly endowed with necessary free will. Choice is everything. Our glory and our agony.

All violence perpetrates increasing whirls of karma, reifies the negation of experience, condemning the perpetrator to ceaseless reincarnations, ceaseless pain, endless accretions of matter. Notice that I use the word perpetrator, rather than person. This is a crucial point for Jainism: ALL organisms possess a soul that is evolving towards a condition of non-violence, a state of general, non-exclusive bliss. An organism that has by chance become a human being finds himself momentarily fraught with a peculiar

mental circumstance, namely, a problematic, restless self-con-
sciousness. That person has become himself as the result of many
previous births. He might have been a lion (Mahavira was a lion
before he was a human), or a cockroach, or his enemy whom he
slayed self-defensively in battle. However he got to be who he is,
whatever violence he may have committed in the past, none of it
matters now: The original soul can be reacquired. It has left traces
in consciousness. And when you are aware of that, and act accordingly, then you are a Jain. You can wipe that slate clean, renounce
the vast molasses of ephemeral attachments and desires, and com-
mence—from this moment—upon a road of total affirmation
(astikya). There is joy in restraint, a life of true significance that
can result from the alleviation of another's misfortune. And one
does not have to be a human being to initiate that relief. Not only
do the Jains know this to be true in theory, but from having
observed the animal kingdom, with its record of partnerships and
symbiosis, universal kin altruism, mothering behavior, socializa-
tions, and flocking strategies.

But bliss, by itself, is not the goal, nor the re-attainment of a
pure soul. Relief of nature is the goal, though this 'equation'
results from a number of consciously avowed inferences: that all
organisms possess an individual soul (as stated, jiva); that there is
great beauty, dignity, and purpose to the soul; that it is immortal,
immaterial but vulnerable to material influences (i.e.violence);
that consciousness is capable—in its highest mode—of acquitting
the soul of its jeopardy; and that this process is accomplished
through the systematic elimination of violence.

The end result is a world that is happy both in spirit, in consciousness, and in body. A world that is enlightened *(kevalajnana)*.

The soul of a bug has the same immortal rights and potential
for enlightenment as any human being. The soul needn't have
anything to do with the *pudgala-skandha* (the aggregate of matter)
in which it is contained. Soul is soul. Ethereal, uncapturable, like
the Tao. Or like a spark, with equal power to ignite a candle or a
whole forest. But there is a thin line between the freedom of the
soul, and the vaguely defined point at which the corporeal himsa,

the denigration of body, drags the soul down into *samsara*, subverting its purity for another round of reincarnation.

Uniquely, Jainism perceives life—the earth and every one of its beings—to be of equal worth to the human. The compassion *(anukampa)* that is born of this revelation is the first step towards rectifying the samsara, or endless unhappiness, that assails all organisms. Aware of the underlying syndrome, unselfish in his cultivation of a pantheistic inviolability, the Jain aspirant resolves to right all trauma, to erect a wilderness area around each soul that is sacrosanct. This hallowed volition is the joy and purpose of human existence, say the Jains; the highest art form; the beginning and end of all aesthetic appreciation.

In an important sense, the soul should be treated like an endangered species. Ecologists know that the only salvation for a species is the protection of the entire biome in which it dwells. That interconnectedness, a similitude of biochemistry, succeeds or fails according to the non-interference prescribed by one species whose members currently find themselves in the awkward and dangerous position as shepherds on earth.

We have it in our power to drag down all other species in an orgy of perverted karma, or to stop bothering them, killing them, driving them to extinction in so many ways—from sheer butchery to the more subtle appropriation of whole ecosystems. With our own souls utterly dependent upon the cornucopia of life around us (which *we alone* are wiping out—forever!—at the current rate of several species per day) the Jain insights into karma, and the possibilities for liberation, are remarkably timely. Here is a way of life that prompts and coddles every wild, and every refined soul; a source of universal salvation that strikes at the heart of ecological science. Remarkably, it is also an art form.

CHAPTER FIVE

Aesthetic Subtleties

JAIN LYRICAL POETRY, PROSE, PAINTING, sculpture, and architecture, have excelled at expressing these ecological concepts. Her art is fiercely original, pictorials executed with an uncannily minimalist abstraction, a pure and shorn design; sculpture scraped—rather than chiselled—from white marble; philosophy frequently expressed in poetic riddles and verse; a whole universe of moral exhortation and touching anecdote. In addition, Jain pilgrimage constitutes a major tradition within India.

Entire mountains have been set aside for Jain temple complexes, such as those at Satrunjaya and Girnara, where pilgrims—sometimes numbering in the thousands—have come barefoot century after century, climbing several thousand vertical feet to the white, radiant summits, for purposes of paying tribute to the ideals of their religion. Nearly all of the twenty four tirthankaras achieved moksha, ultimate deliverance, atop mountains, and the Jains have duly enshrined these particular peaks—as well as their myriad pilgrimages to such sacred spots (*nirvana-bhumis*)—in their thoughts, philosophy, and way of life.

The countless cloudy-white shrines and temples of Palitana atop Satrunjaya beckon the far-winding pilgrim like a cold platter of fresh fruits on a balmy afternoon. Many of the pilgrims arrive by foot, all the way from Ahmedabad a few hundred kilometers away. This the focal point for more than a millenium of sacred interactions on the Gujarat Peninsula.

The mountain is enlivened, children scampering upwards in a delirium of bare feet, dazzled eyes, past fire-bright cactus, and the lowing cattle that freely saunter hither and yon. The effect is one of soft pastorale filling the air. In addition, there is the odd bamboo palanquin bearing the old and infirm to the upper ethereal realms. Locals pick up extra money carrying these heaven-happy loads.

The sun rises on this incomparable aerie of sanctity which looms far above the Arabian Sea. The hundreds of acres of summital white marble, cast in exquisite courtyards, temples, and gleaming statuary, teem with pilgrims, many of whom wear garlands of jasmine. Thousands of birds flutter by in the thermals. Crickets and myriad scents evanesce. The senses are filled with an indescribable purity.

By late afternoon, I recline against a white slab, adjoining a wall of lustrous stone sculpture, lulled into temporary dreaming. Alone in the impervious shadows of blossoming oleanders. By night fall, the cool descending winds impart a strange confidence that Palitana is *alive;* that the entire sanctuary is like a cosmic radio antenna receiving the message of ahimsa from the very spheres. This gentle and encompassing introversion, the very fact of Palitana, is a unique and everlasting achievement of Jain artistry; the outgrowth of a robust philosophy.

At Mt. Abu, the two thirteenth-century temples of Dilwara, designed by the great master builders Vastupala and Tejapala, present what are undoubtedly the greatest sculptured structures in the world. Workmen were paid in gold according to the weight of marble powder they had scraped off. One small piece of a single column was said to have cost several thousand ruppees. The detailed workmanship and minute layers of sensuality inculcated in the downsloping eaves of the Vimala-vasahi temple, with its so-called *ranga-mandapa* ceiling, overpower the senses. Glorious figures, intimate congeries of animal life of an almost incomprehensible beauty, egress from dream to incarnation, becoming more real by the moment, until all of Abu enters the artistic witness and becomes the entire universe.

Until way past midnight, seated inside the temple complex, my only real companions the moonlight, the wind, and the marble, I could peacefully have died in that communion. It's a feeling I've had standing before Giorgione's *La Tempesta* at the Venice Academia, at the Ryoan-ji sand garden in Kyoto, or in front of Vermeer's *Artist In His Studio* at the Vienna Kunsthistorische Museum. But at Abu there is a greater inheritance than mere aethestic consummation. There is the achievement of what I might as well term the *ethical point.* By this I mean that starting place, that clean slate, from whence life is subsequently possible. We flounder much, or all of our lives, bereft of a compass reading, lost at sea, not even knowing what we're looking for, let alone how to get there. Certainly Vermeer and Giorgione, as well as the two landscape architects who signed their name to one of the stones at Ryoan-ji, impart spectacular courage and revelation. But the way of life is left up to the observer. An *ethical point* goes further, still. It proclaims more than a Venetian tradition, or one genius in Delft; even more than the exquisite connoisseurship of Zen landscape. Reflecting an entire historical phenomenon, this particular point of which I speak is the key to reading a treasure map. And these salient, requisite points can be deciphered throughout the hegemony of Jain art and thought.

At the six tenth century caves of Ellora, a bumpy fifteen-hour road from Bombay, Jain frescos and sculpture, elevated up along the sheer escarpments, tunneling into the receptive earth, portray dozens of seated tirthankaras in cool, darkly lit meditation, as well as the earliest sculpted Jain mendicant, Gommatesvara Bahubali, son of the first Tirthankara, standing motionless, in peaceful meditation, vines growing up his legs, ant piles forming at his feet.

Elsewhere, Bahubali's nude likeness was carved out of a single 57-foot high granite rock in the year 983 A.D. He stands atop the Indragiri Hill at Sravanabelgola, near Mysore, in Karnataka State. Ant hills are depicted, as well as *madhavi*—creepers ascending the statue's legs and thighs. Near the shoulders, the vines break out into flower and berries. Bahubali's restful pose is known as *khadgasana*, a stance encompassing total tranquility, concentration, joy. As A. Ghosh points out in his monumental three volume *Jaina Art And Architecture*,[57] the Bahubali carving is predominantly three-dimensional, in the round. No other massive rock carving in the world—whether Ramses, or the Buddhas of Bamiyan—can claim to such perspective.

It was at Sravanabelgola that Bhadrabahu, the great Jain sage of the early fourth and late third-centuries B.C., is alleged to have fasted to death. [Of important note, Bhadrabahu came to Sravanabelgola along with the emperor Candragupta Maurya, allegedly a converted Jain ascetic, as well as many other lay Jains during a disastrous famine in the north. This twelve year migration would result in the tandem evolution of the two principle sects of Jainism—Digambara and the Shvetambara—both of whom trace their mendicant lineage to Mahavira and the earlier Tirthankaras.]

Most of the hundreds of Jain temples throughout India contain sculptures of Mahavira, like the spectacular edifice of Tirupparuttikkunra in Tamil Nadu. Such statuary plays a critical role in the daily life of Jain piety. The layman and monk recite the *Panca Namaskara*—the most basic Jain prayer—before the sculpture, in the sacred Jain language:

"I bow to the enlightened souls, I bow to the liberated souls, I bow to religious leaders, I bow to religious teachers. I bow to all the monks in the world." (*Namo arihantanam, Namo siddhanam, Namo ayariyanam, Namo uvajjhayanam. Namo loe savva sahunam.*)

The devotee walks around the image, and then performs *puja*, washing the image with milk, water, sandlewood and saffron, arranges grains of rice on the temple floor in a symbolic swastika (in reference to the four types of rebirth), places three dots of sand

(Right Faith, Right Knowledge and Right Conduct—the so-called *ratnatraya)* at the top of the little pictogram, then another dot with a crescent, representing the Jain version of nirvana, or absolute ahimsa, above that. The image is not worshipped. It is simply the focus for meditation.[58] This is important: there is no idolatry, no worship of any kind in Jainism. Worship, they insist, invites the arrogance of power, tyranny, exploitation.

The dozens of Jain monastic libraries, or *bhandaras*, commissioned and collected hundreds of illustrated manuscripts throughout the ages. Paintings were done first on talipot or palmyra palm, on thin wooden covers, or patlis, and then on paper.[59] This tradition reached its zenith in western India during the fourteenth and fifteenth centuries. By far the most frequently illuminated manuscript was that of the *Kalpasutra*, the eighth chapter of the fourth *Chedasutra* text known as *Dashashrutaskandha*, ascribed by the Shvetambara tradition to Bhadrabahu.

Executed in striking colors—red, or blue on black, gold on ultramarine, lush oranges, vibrant yellows, cubist proportions, abstracted figures of striking simplicity, energetic lines, austere gazes, dabs of collyrium on the fish-eyes, two dimensional profiles that are attractive, but not seductive, quaint floral arrangements, a proliferation of animals, cosmological symbology, some Chinese and Persian landscape influence—the paintings will, with sufficient concentration, unleash the sensation of pure mendicancy. Fourteen of the symbols concern the dreams which Mahavira's first, and second mother had during the descent, and subsequent transferral of his embryo from the beautiful Devananda to the even more alluring Trishala. Those symbols include an ocean, a lake, a celestial abode, the Sun and the Moon, auspicious objects, a flame, an elephant, lion and bull, a garland of flowers, and the anointing of the goddess Shri, who—throughout India—was always recognized as the Mother Goddess of Earth, India's native Gaia.[60]

There is a presentiment of uncanny comfort to be derived from these uncluttered visions; a whole *Weltanschauung* that dates directly to the example set by Mahavira, the twenty three tirthankaras before him (*Jina charita*), and the substance of ahimsa. These are topics dealt with in the text of the Kalpasutra.[61]

Acarya Bhadrabahu's book of 1200 verses was actually one of many which Bhadrabahu had committed to memory, when manuscripts were being lost because of the major famine that disrupted life in India, the Jain community not excluded, during Bhadrabahu's time. As mentioned earlier, Jain monks and nuns must rest during the period of the summer monsoons. The Kalpasutra examines the conduct appropriate during this period and in so doing, posits general principles applicable to the whole realm of compassion and attentiveness.

The veneration of such paintings is part of the religious liturgy and has its own abundant rules: *svadhyaya* (study), *dhyana* (concentration on a single object), *anuprekshas* (the twelve themes of meditation).[62] Among these latter subjects are such reflections as karmic influx, the vast menagerie of hapless organisms that can not benefit from viewing such art, and the helplessness of beings in the face of death. Anuprekshas is also known as *bhavanas* (yearning thoughts or aspirations). The dozen such categories of thought have been assembled over the Jain eons to help foster self-control. One of them contains a verse, meant to be repeated first thing every morning. The translation reads,

"O, Lord may my self be such that it may have love for all living beings, joy in the meritorious, unstinted sympathy and compassion for the distressed, and tolerance towards the perversely inclined."[63]

Art stemming from such sentiment has its own reason-for-being, and this is clearly observable throughout Jain aesthetics. There are, in addition, four *shukladhyana*, or pure trances, in which a particular kind of intense concentration upon physical existence may result in the yearned-for elimination of passion.[64] Keep in mind that passion, according to the Jains, leads frequently (though not necessarily) to violence, and thus to pain. The art is to be created and viewed in a passionless state, a benign, neutral accord that appreciates, without exaggerating, the importance of the image, as a messenger of moral lessons. It is, of course, an altogether different approach to aesthetics than that which is normally associated with works of art, not only in the west, but in other Indian traditions.

At stake, in Jainism, is the highest pleasure of all: the end of suffering. It is also important to remember that the great Jain sages themselves, such as Mahavira, are not to be venerated, according to this doctrine of passionless pleasure. Rather, the *ideals* espoused by real people, the Tirthankaras, like Mahavira, are what constitute the proper focus.[65] In Jainism, life models itself after art.

Jains believe that the creation of such art—the sculptures, the temples, the paintings—are "the noblest of worldly activities."[66] In Jinasena's late eighth-century epic poem, the *Adipurana* (which has been hailed as "an encyclopaedia of the Digambara religion")[67] there are depictions of six rapturous seasons with beauteous moons and dazzling suns, amorous gatherings and titillating romance. But there are also chapters on governance, even town planning. It is a complete world picture, lending additional credence to a philosophical stance that encompasses all views, all knowledge, in order to more effectively forge an artistic, ethical realism.

The universe is nature; the human reaction is art, art devoted to alleviating suffering. Within these interlocked fields is all hope, effort, passionless passion, all morality, all Jainism.

From as early as the first century A.D., the Digambara scholar, Kundakunda, described the *Nishcaya Naya*—a transcendental view—as fundamental to any ethical achievement. Kundakunda went on to explain in his work *Samayasara*, that the transcendent view, or viewpoint, pertains to the essential and non-karmic nature of the soul. Kundakunda, Samantabhadra, and many hundreds of years later, Amrtacandra each arrived at the same conclusion, based upon unequivocal statements in the Acaranga Sutra: that this transcendent soul, or self, is the quintessence of ahimsa; that all living beings are the same; that nirvana is ahimsa.[68] And

that the aesthetic experience has the power to convey this revelation. Indeed, for Samantabhadra, the total practice of ahimsa is
"equivalent to the realization of the highest self."[69]

In his *Moksha Pahuda*, Kundakunda described this aesthetic
revelation as leading the world to a condition known as *Jivan-
mukta*, the divine on earth; without analogy, the final condition of
bliss.[70] It is this universal truth which underscores the Jain
premise of *anekantavada*, a doctrine of manifold aspects, multiple
viewpoints, non-absolutist comprehension, allowing for that
which is the other, beyond, outside normal expression. There are
hidden corners, dark aeries, wonderful abodes in the paintings of
the Kalpasutra—places where consciousness has detected inti-
mations of true ahimsa, free and wild. They are rare moments in
Jainism, the living expressions of a laser-like focus which has
achieved its mark.

In 1968, an unknown manuscript by the Digambara artist,
Amrtacandra (tenth-century), was translated and brought to publication by Professor Padmanabh S. Jaini. Entitled *Laghutattvasphota*, this marvelous work of philosophical poetry, steeped in
riddles and descriptive passages, re-affirms the *nishcaya* (non-
conventional, transcendent) view as leading the aspirant back (or
forward) to his original soul. It is important to note that the jiva of
every being contains an undamageable purity, however affecting
its karman impediments. What this means of course is that Jainism is a religion of optimists, contrary to the fatalistic overtones.
While the religion posits pain in the world as one of its starting
points, it counters by recognizing this myriad joy which is the
inalienable fact of every soul.

In one characteristically Jainist fusion of physics and philosophy, invoking the tirthankaras, Amrtacandra writes of a bril-
liance, an "unparalleled light" that "appears like a painting that
has been blurred by a flood of water..." and goes on to describe
"the mass of your light, whose form is knowledge..." and which
dispenses with the conventional "net of distinctions (that we normally make) between existence, non-existence, etc., (by giving

us a glimpse of infinite consciousness)."[71] What a marvelous inti-
mation of the divine; cryptic, beguiling, science and sensation
wedded to a purpose greater than ourselves.

The "etc." of the above passage is no mere convenience of
syntax, some casual reference to an unintoned enumeration of
attributes. Rather, it is the Jain way of noting an inexpressible
addition, something way out, light years away from our mundane
attachment to words which bind us, like karma. Beyond that
"etc."—reminiscent of god's abbreviated universe as couched in
the Hebraic letters YAWH—is the glorious "mass of light" which
breaks through the darkness, lending purity and peace at long
last to all being.

Thus, light becomes energy; art metamorphoses into action.
One defends the family, the loved ones, the wilderness, with no
weapon other than aesthetic passion, mystical purity, inner goodness. Artistic conscience is the means toward an end.

A Religion of Restraints

BECAUSE HUMAN BEINGS ARE CARELESS, there is a hierarchy of consecration, born of the pragmatic, throughout Jainism. It is, therefore, less karmically heinous to kill an ant accidently, than it is to commit a premeditated murder. Eating a fruit with many seeds is terrible, but less so than eating meat. Seeds propagate life, therefore the consumption of certain high seed-bearing fruits is unnecessarily destructive, since by doing so the taking of one fruit in fact takes many. Nevertheless, those fruit have only one sense, that of feeling, whereas the water buffalo, or beef cow has five senses. Most cows and water buffalos die of a natural death in India, usually from malnutrition. But the Hindu worships these animals, and Indian society places great emphasis upon dung patties for fuel, humus and building materials, as well as the buffalo's milk. It is too much of a luxury to eat cattle. Nevertheless, say the Jains, when it has died its meat is still prohibited because of the millions of micro-organisms which necessarily take up the carcass as a place of cozy habitation. To eat the animal would kill off those microbiotic communities, as well as the larger, maggot-sized organisms, whom the Jains also respect.

In addition, the eating of such meat, even though the animal may have died a natural death, reminds the consumer that he is eating an animal. Such a thought is intolerable in Jainism, the basis for an inevitable escalation of conceptual ill-will. Concept defines practice. Practice quickly inundates the jiva with karma. And karma dictates the personality and its desinty, from the child to the adult. There is no other ontology.

Buddhism never went so far as to ascribe this level of inviolability to a dead carcass, let alone the *idea* of a dead carcass. Nor to sexual intercourse. For the Jains, sexual desire on the part of a monk is deeply regrettable, but ejaculation is akin to genocide, in that a few hundred million sperm will die. Such utilitarian convictions may seem fiendishly academic, or impractical, or absurd, even for a monk. But in fact, such comprehensive proscriptions are at the heart of ahimsa, which is a total philosophy, without ideological compromise. Again, the *logic* is unerring.

Both the layman and monk will ordinarily fall far short of achieving total ahimsa. That is understood, and that is why ahimsa was broken down into categories that could be rendered more manageable in a household, or more easily monitored in a monastery. For example, there is *samkalpajahimsa*, violence which is intentional; and *arambhajahimsa*, occupational violence; and there is *virodhihimsa*, violence to counteract violence. The distinctions strike of legal nuances that have since come to mold the common sense jurisprudence of courts throughout the world.

For example, transgressions are not only defined according to whether they were committed consciously or not, with care or not, with the intention to hurt, or not; but precisely *how* consciously, *how* carelessly, *how* hurtfully. Within each of these zones of violence, there are innumerable shades, qualifications, sub-categories of human experience. And none of them escape the scrutiny of Jain psychoanalysis. It is this calculated odyssey towards empathy, this fervent analysis and daily exorcism of harm that so accounts for Jainism's abiding importance.

The orthodox canons, and the *sravakacaras*, those breviaries for the layman, have covered every conceivable activity of a human day, at least in ancient India. In the earliest two Digambara texts, namely, *Mulacara* and *Pravacanasara*, the monks were exhorted to conduct themselves with perfect asceticism. This meant no "unhealthy gossip," the pulling out of one's hair every six months (*kesa-loca*), not cleaning the teeth, taking meals while standing upright, remaining naked, sleeping on the ground, in the forest, bearing all miseries, eating little, and cultivating love *(mettim bhavehi)*.[72] This latter ordinance, nestled within the vortex of self-mortifications, underlies the affirmative approach to nature which is, in the end, Jainism.

For the monk and layperson alike, there are three principles which constitute the basis for all subsequent ethical delineations: right belief, right knowledge, and right conduct. Within these general phrases, every feature of experience is accounted for—from walking to laughing, from fear to humility. There is no verb, no adverb, no noun or pronoun that escapes the Jain moral hegemony. The 'earth,' 'water,' 'fire,' 'wind,' 'plant' and 'power of movement' are each considered realms of life, each one vulnerable to pain, pain that is augmented by human over-indulgence, immorality, or sheer inadvertence. To correct this perpetual infliction, the life of a Jain monk is obsessed with the myriad vows of *vrata*, restraint. The layperson is equally concerned, though less obsessed, with *anu-vrata*, lesser restraints. The monastic orthodoxy underscores every Jain householder and serves as a comforting reminder, if not a noble temptation, throughout his or her life.

There is, additionally, a condition of 'temporary asceticism' which combines the two approaches. The layperson meditates in the presence of an ascetic (the meditation known as *samayika)* and during this brief period he undertakes to cast aside his former self and adopt the full complement of vratas. It is, of course, unlikely that any layperson is even familiar with all of the vratas, but it is the ahimsa vratas that are primary—the immediate cessation of any harmful thoughts and activities. Such remission is not difficult, and it is difficult. But if we can control our dreams, then we can sleep in ahimsa. If we can control our waking thoughts—but totally—and sit quietly on a cleansed surface, touching no living being, including oneself, then this too might be described as momentary ahimsa. (In the final analysis, the monk knows that even his passive body is an interior battle ground where cells live and die, where illness attacks and is counter-attacked. He is willing to forbear this realization in the service of a greater need, a more widespread alleviation of suffering that may result from his own pertinacity and love.)

Just as those "two minutes" of acrimony can suffer exponential multiplication throughout an undisciplined life, so too, conversely, a few moments of temporary asceticism may be sufficient to engender the conviction of a lifetime. Those two minutes, possitively approached, become the ethical point for all future behavior.

Love was always at the heart of the message promulgated by the ancient Jain sages. A love of life that would inspire the lay votaries to achieve great dreams, to fulfill life's highest possibilities. The severity of Jain asceticism is strictly oriented towards that love—not towards renouncing it. This is an important point, to be sure: Jain asceticism is about the human capacity for love, and by inference, about nature's own ability to have feeling, to share gentle thoughts, to act accordingly. The soul of nature transmigrates into the soul of the monk. And this scintillating relationship is inbred within the community. Nature does not play havoc with the Jains. Rather, it fosters their thinking, which in turn—reciprocally—gives back to nature her first, loving impulses. Non-injury to life is self-replicating in the Jains. And thus, this religion has sought to engineer a perpetual biological renascence, from the soul, to the psyche, to the external world, and back again. This is the cycle of rebirth, the passion of all art, and the one hope of the future that I can imagine: a spiritual ecology.

Temporary asceticism also intimates the vast range of abuse that human life doles out all around it, short of the love described above, suggesting an enormous effort that will be required to intercede on behalf of gentleness. Our normal picture of peace and harmony may well be shot through with oblivious injury. A French

Impressionist picnic in the country can be devastating to hundreds, perhaps thousands of insects and plants.

The Kalpasutra goes into some detail on the nature of eight of these organisms: living beings, fungi, seeds, sprouts, flowers, eggs, habitats, and moisture particles. Five different colored creatures are described, as well as ant-holes, furrows, cavities, the base of palm trees, wasps' nests, the eggs of spiders and lizards, ants and chameleons, and five types of particles—dew, frost, fog, hailstones and small water-particles. Monks and nuns are reminded to "remain constantly alert in order to detect them" lest they harm the beings contained therein. Such adumbrations combine the elements of a dozen disciplines, from biology to ethics, stipulating all that is frail and vulnerable in nature.[73]

The Sthanakavasi and Terapanthi sub-sects of the Shvetambaras will not even breathe unfiltered air. They wear masks, known as *muh-patti*, so as to protect insects from getting in the mouth and dying, and to curb any verbal improprieties, as well as maintaining a balance between the inside and outside temperature of the mouth, thus assuring a minimum of harm to bacteria on the tongue and palate.

While there are but five principal anuvratas—*ahimsa* (non-violence), *satya* or *sunrita* (truth), *asteya* (not stealing), *brahmacarya* (sexual abstinence), and *aparigraha* (nonpossession), there are also fourteen steps or *gunasthana* (rungs) of the ethical ladder, each of which in turn comprise dozens of partial steps. One step at a time, that is the idea, the latitude by which people can go on living in spite of themselves. There are the eleven *pratimas*—stages of spiritual progress for the layman; the eight *mulagunas*, or basic restraints, which include the renunciation of all meat, alcohol, honey and figs; there are the restrictions with respect to enjoyment, activity, fasting, charity and meditation.[74]

Why alcohol, one might ask? Simply because intoxication leads to passion, exerts malevolent effects on a person's health, thinking and behavior; and—through the act of fermentation—leads to the deaths of countless organisms. Why honey? Because, say the Jains, other myriads of micro-organisms are destroyed when honey is pressed out of the comb. With respect to figs and many other fruits of the *ficus* genus (particularly, in India, the gular, anjir, banyan, pipal and pakar), there are innumerable life-bearing seeds that go to waste, which could otherwise have served to propagate creation.

Extending from this logic, or vow, are other restrictions with respect to the use of luxury items, nearly all cosmetics, fancy soaps, oils and unguents among them. However, a house-holder is permitted to massage the feet of a wandering ascetic and help to heal any ailment he may have. This may be the only spiritually-sanctioned massage in the history of religions. [75]

The eleven pratimas constitute a formidable basis for daily life among lay Jains, or quiet converts to Jainism. They are:

Darshana = a right attitude.

Vrata = observance of the Jain vows (anuvratas, guna-vratas and siksa-vratas).

Samayika = introspection, meditation.

Proshadhopavasa = various degrees of motivated fasting.

Sacitta-tyaga = observance of all dietary proscriptions; carefulness with respect to where one walks and what one drinks. No unboiled water. No trampling of grass or other plants.

Ratribhojana-tyaga = No food or drink at night; no sexual intercourse during the day; sexuality at night only for the purpose of procreation.

Brahmacarya = celibacy.

Arambha-tyaga = limitation of possessions to bare essentials. The rest should be given to one's children and to charities. Renunciation of all jobs, and of one's profession.

Parigraha-tyaga = becoming more and more solitary, living in a temple, reading scriptures, taking food only at midday, food given to him by other Jains, of their own accord. Without any possessions, even essentials.

Anumati-tyaga = no more attachments to family, food, likes or dislikes.

Uddishtha-tyaga = goes to an ascetic to take vows; will live as an ascetic, clad only in a loincloth; head shaved (his hair pulled out), bare-footed. Food taken in his palms once a day, the result of quiet, dignified begging. Food must not be accepted if it was specially prepared for him (that would be interfering).[76]

Once having become an ascetic, there are 28 *Mula-gunas*, or ascetical vows, that must be continually embraced, and all of them encompassed within the broadest definition of ahimsa. The vows stipulate care—care in everything one does (*samitis*), from begging, to walking, even care in the observance of the call of nature. One must forsake bathing, self-adornment of any kind, and sleep on bare ground in caves and remote forests. Careful behavior is the first creed instilled in Jain children. By the time the acculturated Jain has become an adult, or is ready to contemplate an advanced *pratima*, the long-time indoctrination has facilitated a gentle transition to increasingly ascetical vows. The approach to liberation is a humane one, ever mindful of its reason for being: the protection of other life forms.

Throughout this entire process of increasing renunciation and restraint *(virati)*, there is a conspicuous absence of any moral guardians in the community. There are no den-mothers, watchdogs, policemen, let alone witch-hunts or inquisitions. No priests, no hymns, no divine prayers. This spiritualism is strictly a private, practical affair. There *are* Jain festivals—lots of them—and social commingling on a daily basis in the temples, where images of Jain sages are adored and respected. But there is no enforcement, no fear of damnation hanging over a compulsory life. Nor is there guilt (in the Freudian sense), confession, or sin, for that matter. Jains never proselytize. A religion free of god, they have only themselves to blame.

Whereas the Holocaust poses an illogic of monstrous proportions—given the Judeo-Christian premise of a god, the generic promise of a latent humanism in all men—Jainism, while equally stricken with the anxiety of being human, of thus fostering every conceivable contradiction, is not similarly gripped by the insoluble existentialism of a post-Nietzschean world. And because its memory of pain has not paralyzed it with suspicion and doubt, it is free to be active, to start fresh each day, even in the face of every impediment and adversity.

By breaking down each act to its psychological and biological constituents, the Jains have adopted surgical masks and gloves and ethically dissected the world in order to save it. So that in actual fact, the tyranny of self-control is nothing less than radical will. The Jains realize that their vows did not touch a Hitler. But Jainism has never stressed intervention. Instead, Jains rely upon the philosophy of individual modesty; of individuals working out their own non-violent destinies. Given individual personalities and vicissitudes, no predictions are set forth about collective behavior. There is no philosophy of the masses in Jainism.

The arena of possible injuries and wrongdoings that is fundamental to individuals and their erratic behavior, and out of which this religion of healers hopes to attain psycho-somatic salvation, extends far beyond any easily apprehensible litany. Amitagati, the tenth century Digambara commentator, reckoned that there were 108 primary forms of human violence. Several years later, the Shvetambara critic, Devagupta, counted 243 *bhangas*, or intentional trangressions. Other medieval critics perceived even more complex networks of injury. [77] The eleventh century Digambara philosopher, Amrtacandra assessed the harm caused by desire and anger; while the massively erudite Shvetambara Hemacandra, in his twelfth century treatise entitled *Yoga-shastra*, examined the violence committed by several Hindu deities and asked with disgust how it was that such murderers could be worshipped. There were categories of untruth pertaining to cows, virgins, land; himsa divined in the very act of tactlessness, evil brooding, or harmful counsel. (On this latter point, a Jain lawyer, for example, could never defend someone whom he knew to be guilty.) [78]

There were short and long-term restraints, lists of dietary taboos that took in to account even those organisms in the stomach (*gandolaka*). The *abhaksyas*, as they were called, those strictures pertaining to food, gave the practice of ahimsa a particularly family-oriented impetus: non-violence began in the home, around the dinner table (dinner being served always before sunset). For the monk, the best food was that which was free from any living thing. For the householder, the ideal diet consisted of a few basic staples, rice and vegetables and simple fruit.

The same simplicity adhered with respect to professions. Because the forbidden livelihoods included any work involving animals, animal by-products, large-scale transport, the use of fire or water or earth, this had to have made life intrinsically difficult for the average individual in ancient India. It has not gotten easier with time. In fact, the chain of transgressions has become far more obtuse, cause and effect increasingly obscured. We read that animals in Alaska have been deliberately killed in order to bolster the government's case against an oil company, and feel utterly helpless, bereft, somehow distantly implicated in the crime. Events and distraught individuals in the Middle East that unleashed the worst oil spill in human history, killing millions, perhaps billions of defenseless organisms, further complicate a syndrome of guilt and passive implication. We can not undo the tragedies, or sever the links which have bound us to our automobiles and thus to the catastrophes of a Prince William Sound or Persian Gulf. Such bondage is both cerebral and physical. You can do penance in any number of ways, by writing a letter, signing a petition, placing a strategic phone call, volunteering in a clean-up operation, giving a donation, getting politically involved, voting. There are similarities with the past.

For example, in 1582 the Mogul emperor Akbar asked the Jain monk Hirvijaya Suri to come to his court for purposes of philosophical discussion. The monk then persuaded Akbar to implement days of the calendar year when any and all killing of animals— whether for purposes of eating, hunting, or ritual sacrifice—would be outlawed. The Jain monk would have preferred Akbar to outlaw all killing all of the time. But Akbar loved hunting. The monk struck a political compromise. Finesse is understood by Jainism.[79]

Ethical surgery, non-intervention. This is a philosophical tightrope. Yet in reality, the results are impressive.

CHAPTER SEVEN

Pragmatics

REMARKABLY, MOST OF THE ANCIENT injunctions are altogether applicable today. At an Arab animal market in Ahmedabad, I watched as rupees furiously exchanged hands, merchants screaming at one another over the disparate bleating of the thousands of sheep which had been corralled, ensnared in wire, sold, thrown into trucks, and driven off to various slaughter houses. Two hundred and fifty animals were tossed into each vehicle, like luggage. The temperature was over one hundred degrees. The animals had no water, and would never drink again. Packed like sardines, they would be driven in some cases hundreds of miles to have their heads chopped off, their meat divided. Jains will frequent such markets, which are scattered all over India—all over the world—to save the animals, paying nearly any price. The animals are then treated like orphans, dispatched to various panjorapors, and reared in comfort. This too is where Jainism begins. It is the one form of interference inherent to Jain ethics.

As with the Bible and its readers, so too there has been constant Jain exegesis, modernization. Whether for judges or radiator manufacturers. Hotel owners, pharmacists, or physicians. In the old days, it was forbidden to ride on a bullock cart, not just because it is considered violent to keep a pet, let alone to have put a harness on his back, or because farming in general was always discouraged, but because the wheels of the bullock cart would inevitably kill nigoda, or ekendriya, the smallest life forms. In the modern world, bullock carts are still killers, but so are airplanes. Monks are not allowed to fly in them. The *ekendriya jiva* (also called *Sthavar Jivas)* have only one sense organ (*Sparsa-Indriya,* the sense of touch) but four powers, or *pranas,* namely, touch, body, the power of exhalation and inhalation. In addition, there are six classes of ekendriya—*prithvikaya,* the stones, salts and diamonds of earth; *apakaya,* such as rain and dews and fogs; *teukaya* (or *tejaskayika),* organisms that dwell within fire; *vayukaya jivas* that inhabit hurricanes and cyclones, monsoons and trade winds; *vanaspatikaya,* which take up residence in trees; and finally *sadharana,* certain types of vegetables like potatoes or onions or garlic which grow under the soil.[80]

Most Jains admit that the accidental killing of the ekendriya can not be avoided, though monks are less sanguine about such accidents. But all Jains—however 'westernized'—actively refrain from harming the *trasa jivas,* those souls with more than one sense, beginning with the *dvindriya,* such as worms and leeches. These creatures both touch and taste and are duly protected. *Trindriya* organisms which have three senses—touch, taste, and smell (such as moths, ants and lice) are even more sacrosanct.

The hierarchy of organisms enlarges with four, then five sensed beings. All are inviolate, equal, adrift in a planetary puzzle of spiritual co-involvement that is frequently summarized with reference to "worms, ants, black-bees, (and) human beings" in that order.[81]

What is ironic, but not surprising, is the modern success story which is Jainism. In ancient times, according to stone inscriptions left by donors to Jain causes, we can glean a sense of the professions adopted by lay residents of the Jain center of Mathura: merchant, trader, jeweller, iron trader, goldsmith, caravan-guide, per-fume-seller, smith, courtesan, dancer, reciter, village headman and cotton dealer.[82] All of these occupations were specifically non-violent. And all of them were considered to foster lucrative employment. Today, Jains have maintained their status as one of the richest communities in India and this attribution can be indis-putably related to the fact that the professions to which their reli-gion has restricted them are valuable ones: environmental clean-up, computer sciences, law, publishing, education, all those activities which pose a minimal impact on the ecology, and the ecology of the soul. The countless professionals, secular and lay Jains I have had the good fortune to know are successful, vital, and aware. The steps they have taken to minimize violence come directly from the ancient Jain scriptures, and from the marked re-affirmation which the Jain community conveys to its adherents.

It has been pointed out that the one strange omission from those scriptures is any in-depth ethical discussion of warfare, surely one of the more fundamental topics in any analysis of non-violence. Professor Jaini illuminates a single verse by the tenth century Jain scholar, Somadevasuri, indicating that killing, even in a defensive war, should be avoided if at all possible, by the monk, though is pardonable for the layperson. The fact that Jains are not typically born into a *ksatriya* (warfare) caste has meant that they have not normally been called upon to defend their country. Interestingly, all of the tirthankaras *were* of the ksatriya caste, a birthright lending additional weight and authority to their conver-sion to non-violence.

Yet given the Jain denial (in principle) of a caste system, this should not have prevented the Jains from either volunteering, or at least discussing the issues at hand. Professor Jaini perhaps rightly points to this ambivalent silence as the one "serious indict-ment of a tradition so closely associated with the ideal of nonvio-lence."[83] But Professor Jaini has also suggested additional evi-dence indicating a more widespread address of what is recognized to be one of the most difficult of issues in India.[84] As mentioned earlier, lay Jains are offered the possibility of military service, according to the dictates of self-defense. *Asi*, or the sword, is an occupational option under the category of *arambhi-udyami*, in other words, a house-holder's way of surviving. [85]

In the stories surrounding Bahubali, son of the first Tirthankara, Rishabha, many points of military interest have been drawn by Jain scholars. Bahubali's older brother, Bharata, acquired the claim to kingship over ancient India when Rishabha left the throne to become the first Jain mendicant. Bahubali contested his brother's claim, and the king's advisers recommended a personal combat to avoid plunging the whole country into war. Bahubali beat his brother in a wrestling match, but then renounced his plans to become king, embarked on a Jain spiritual path and stood motionless in a meditation that invited plants to invest his legs, and insects to burrow beneath his heels. In this manner Bahubali achieved enlightenment. His legacy is one of valor and subsequent restraint. As Professor Jaini relates, Bharata was applauded for his sense of duty to the territory, his ministers were right in advocating a one-on-one contest to avoid greater bloodshed, and Bahubali's final continence was rewarded with the ultimate attainment. Everyone achieved maturity through careful choice and the adoption of peaceful means to satisfying their goals.

According to the famed first century B.C. Orissan King Kharavela inscriptions, "the first complete historical record of the achievements of a king of ancient India,"[86] Kharavela was both a Jain ruler, and a military victor. But it is significant that there is no mention of his having ever killed an enemy. The conqueror used benign means, apparently, to force the will of his opponents and eventually devoted all of his time to serving Jain monks. Kharavela thus emerges as a model for non-violent military action. Unfortunately, there is a dearth of documentation to illuminate his particular method of negotiation, or non-violent persuasion.

Professor Jaini also relates how Mahavira, in the *Bhagavati-sutra*, was said to have denied any prospect for human rebirth to those who had killed on a battlefield. For those who only killed as an act of self-defense, however, rebirth into *heaven* (though not enlightenment) was possible.[87] It should be noted that the Jains considered the proverbial Mount Olympus, with its multitude of gods (devas) to be of a much less compelling or salutary status to that of moksha. There is no comparison, in fact. Rebirth in heaven was considered regressive, whereas a reincarnation on earth, particularly in human form, more fervently readied the soul for its true purpose.

Mahavira's unambivalent rejection of what in contemporary parlance would be called "first strike" on a battlefield, coupled with his compassion towards those who would kill as a final act of self-defense, is a clear and rational voice at the very heart of Jain military ethics.

There are still other interpretations of the nonetheless restrained discussions concerning warfare in the Jain canons. At least one ancient Jain tribe in Bihar (the Sarakas of Manabhuma), do not even allow the word *slaughter* to be used.[88]

In both Buddhist and Taoist tradition, there is a point at which discourse inherently fails to resolve a difficulty; can not adequately express an underlying assumption that is comprehensive. Silence, or innuendo, or the total orientation of the individual, becomes a fitting response in such instances. Such was the legacy of Lao Tzu, as witnessed in the *Tao Te Ching*. The ideal of conscientious objection hinges upon religious introversion, non-action, or silence. Debate and discourse are not necessarily appropriate to an ethical stance which rejects any climate of antagonism to begin with. In a similar vein, you can not easily use language to transcend language. Apropos of such impasse, Jainism allows for no latitude on the subject of meat-eating. Somadevasuri's simple, if rather cryptic avowal says it all, without having to enunciate the unhappy particulars or gradations: self-defense on the part of the lay-person is, as a last resort, justifiable. The Jains are not pacifists. They actively affirm non-violence. They have staged various protests and provided sanctuary for refugees during wartime. Their position on war can be deduced from the elaborate corpus of rules and insights regarding non-violence in general that makes up their world view. That such relative silence *not* be construed as a weak rationalization, a mere "cop-out" or vacuous gesture, can perhaps best be gauged in its forceful interpretation by Mahatma Gandhi.

Gandhi wasn't actually a Jain. Rather, he was raised under the tutelage of a Jain teacher from the age of seven. His closest friend, the Jain layman Raychandbhai Mehta, exercised an enormous influence on Gandhi. At a communal house in Ahmedabad, Gandhi lived and worked between 1917 and 1933, and there adopted ahimsa as his true religion, along with a host of accompanying vows, the practice of spinning, of chastity, meager possessions, dietary restrictions, and an absolute insistence upon truth in all dealings. These were all Jain precepts to the core. Gandhi was to show how ahimsa could work on the level of an entire nation in the twentieth century.

When workers following Gandhi were beaten at the first sit-down strike at Dharasana in 1930, there were of course skeptics, like George Orwell, who felt justified in saying, 'I told you so.' What he, and General Smuts, and Sir Stafford Cripps and of course King George V and Queen Mary had all ignored, was the power of non-violence. Gandhi interpreted three thousand years of Jainism and came up with *satyagraha*, the civil disobedience of Thoreau, epic fasts, and an ever-present sense of humor through it all. At 73, the emaciated, toothless, old guru tenaciously proved that ahimsa could create a whole nation. Equally important, and fundamental to what the Jains mean when they refer to the inner ahimsa, Gandhi's tactics succeeded in liberating not only India, but England as well. More precisely, the English. Gandhi relieved the guilt of imperialism and showed how compassion could operate between nations. In this respect, he echoed most compellingly the line in the Acaranga Sutra which refers to those who are "turned round in the whirl of pains." [89]

Gandhi's spinning had resulted in a cottage industry that put millions of British fabric workers out of business. When Gandhi visited England and appeared before hordes of angry unemployed Anglo-Saxons, he managed to win them over. His courage, his lucidity, bolstered the underdog in everyone. He returned to

India the utter darling of his former enemies. This too was ahimsa.

Hundreds-of-thousands of Hindus and Muslims massacred each other following India's partition, but Gandhi was true to his Jain beliefs, even up to the very moment of his assassination. He wrote, "Our non-violence is as yet a mixed affair. It limps. Nevertheless, it is the only way."

Acarya Shushil Kumar, leader of the Sthanakavasi Jains, was one of the first monks to fly abroad, in 1975, in order to start a Jain ashram in New Jersey. There were Jains who protested his airplane travel by lying down on the runway at the airport prior to his departure. They argued that airplanes kill organisms (which they do). But Kumar—in the spirit of Gandhi—was insistent upon fostering peace throughout the world.

I spoke with Kumar on the roof of an ashram in New Delhi. He was ardent, forthcoming, concerned with the future:

"Politics has been a dirty game for three thousand years. Man has been fighting and fighting and fighting. Ahimsa is the one system (that can work). If you're ready to fight, then fight with non-violence. You have no other choice. You will have to select one thing: total destruction, or total survival. We have to try. We have to decide. And we have to apply (that decision) to the whole of society."

It was in this spirit that the Kshatriya Prince Nemi long ago renounced his kingdom, in spite of a Brahmin's protests, and stated, "Greater is the victory of him who conquers his only Soul, than of him who conquers thousands of valiant foes in a fierce battle." [90]

The simplicity is perfect. Like the wheel, the zero, the handshake, every revolution contains a seed of pure thought. Jainism does not lose hold of that purity in the mad rush to transform the world; but rather nurtures the seed from within, as one would raise children or cultivate a wild and restless garden.

CHAPTER EIGHT

Blessings

THESE MANY THOUGHTS had crossed my
mind while viewing the simple and
ancient ritual whereby the householders
gave food to the naked Digambara monk
at the temple village of Taranga. It was
their joy and pride to do so. The ascetic
now completed his meal and rejoined his
companion outside. I followed them
upstairs into one of the householders
bungalows, where they intended to rest
and study and meditate during the heat
of the day.

Here then were two luminaries in the
avant-garde of compassion, naked, be-
stowing blessings on little girls, butter-
flies, old men in the village, a feral pig,
monkeys, kokila birds, a tiger and her
cubs up among the cliffs..... Not com-
pletely at peace by any means—how
could they be with the knowledge that
other organisms were in pain all over
India and beyond—but well on their way
towards making a small difference, certainly in the village of Taranga this day.
The ascetics had transformed themselves
with great effort into living, breathing
works of art, humanity, of great inspira-
tion. Thousands of people had greeted

them; thousands more would see them on some hot and dusty road, walking in a controlled fashion, their peacock feathers and gourds by their sides, spreading the message of ahimsa.

I sat briefly with the two ascetics. They chatted in the most friendly and upbeat manner. Who was I? What was I doing at Taranga? From which country did I come? There was nothing self-centered about these two wanderers. Quite to the contrary, their hearts were crying out with love, with fascination and compassion for the whole world. I felt it in the air between us. An archetypal source of strength. A warmth. A hope. It was an amazing feeling—naked tears and the joy of coming home—for which I shall be forever grateful. I have never been the same since that day.

Before leaving, they conferred certain blessings upon me and as we parted they uttered what is one of the most basic salutations in Jainism:

> *"Khamemi sabbajive*
> *sabbe jiva khamantu me*
> *metti me sabbabhuyesu*
> *veram majjha na kenavi"*

("I forgive all beings, may all beings forgive me. I have friendship toward all, malice toward none.")[91]

These events took place some years ago. There is no easy and symmetrical aftermath. No polished coda. Only my rough, aspiring nudity—clothes or no clothes. To remain all-vulnerable; so that the earth's solace and joy can be myself—no longer a stranger in human flesh. That I might give that joy in return.

acarya: head monk
adattadana-viramana: non-stealing
ahampratyaya: self-awareness
ahimsa: non-violence, non-injury, non-harming
ajiva: the material world
alocana: critical self-examination
anagara-dharma: mendicant discipline
ananta-sukha: infinite bliss
anashana: fasting
anekantavada: doctrine of manifold aspects
anukampa: compassion
anupreksha: the twelve reflections
anuvratas: layman's vows (the minor ones)
aparigraha: non-possession
arambhaja-himsa: accidental violence, or violence as the result of a sanctioned occupation
aryika: Digambara nuns
asamyama: non-restraint
asrava: karmic influx, karmic dust
astikya: affirmation
atithi-samvibhaga: sharing with a guest
atman: soul; also self

bandha: karmic bondage
bodhi: enlightenment
bodiya: naked
brahmacari: celibate

caitanya: consciousness

dana: charity
darshana: intuition
dharma: the law
dharma-tirtha: holy path
dhyana: meditation
Digambara: one of two primary Jain sects: sky-clad, naked monks
diksha: initiation
dravya: substance
dravyasrava: karmic inflow

ekendriya: one-sensed being

gunavratas: behavioral restraints

himsa: violence

irya-samiti: care in walking

Jaina: one who follows a Jina
Jina: a Tirthankara, spiritual victor, conqueror of self
Jina-bhavana: jaina temple
jinakalpin: a monk who follows the behavior of Mahavira
jiva: soul
jiva-daya: compassion, empathy and charity
jivanamukti: liberation in this life
jnana: knowledge

kala: time
karma: matter
kasaya: absolute absence of passion
kevalajnana: omniscient knowledge
kevalin: one who has obtained kevalajnana
kriyas: action
kshama: forgiveness
kshanti: forbearance
kshayika-samyak-darshana: true insight through destruction
   of karma

leshya: the color of a soul's relative purity

Mahavira: 24th Tirthankara
mahavrata: the five vows of a mendicant
maitri: universal friendliness
manushya: human being
mohaniya-karma: illusion-fostering karma
moksha: salvation
mrshavada-viramana: non-falsehood
muh-patti: cloth worn over the mouth of Sthanakavasi mendicants
mulagunas: eight basic lay Jain restraints

namaskara-mantra: daily Jain salutation
naya: partial view of reality
nayavada: the doctrine of naya
nigoda: smallest life forms
nirvana: the death of an enlightened one, followed by moksha

parama brahma: the very god(referring to ahimsa)
paramanu: atoms
paramatman: highest soul
parasparopagraho jivanam: interdependence of soul
parigraha: possession

parigraha-viramana: non-possessiveness
Parshvanatha: 23rd Tirthankara
pinchi: a peacock-feather whiskbroom
prajna: wisdom
pranatipata-viramana: non-injury
pratima: eleven rules towards liberation for the layman
pravrajya: renunciation
pudgala: matter, from which karma is engendered
puja: daily consecration, ritual
puranas: sacred texts treating of the Jinas

raga: passion, attachment
ratnatraya: the three jewels of faith, knowledge and conduct

sadhu: mendicant
sadhviji: Shvetambara nun
sallekhana: ritual fasting to death
samatva: sense of kinship and equality with all life forms
samayika: equanimity
samiti: self-regulation
samkalpaja-himsa: premeditated violence
samsara: cycle of transmigration, interflux of souls
samvara: stopping karmic influx, inhibition
samyak-caritra: proper conduct
samyama: restraint
sashtra: scripture
satya: truth
sayogakevalin: spiritual liberation
siddha: liberated soul
siddhi: yogic power
shikshavratas: vows of spiritual discipline
shramana: non-Vedic mendicant, i.e. a Jain
Shvetambara: primary Jaina sect of white robed-monks
syadvada: relativity of truths

tapas: austerity
Tirthankara: Jina
trasa: mobile beings with two or more senses

vairagya: aversion leading to renunciation
vipaka: karmic retribution
virodhi-himsa: injury promulgated in self-defense
vratas: vows

yatra: pilgrimage
yoga: activity

FOOTNOTES

1. *The Jain Declaration On Nature*, by Dr. L. M. Singhvi, presented to His Royal Highness Prince Philip, on 23rd October 1990 at Buckingham Palace, p.7.

2. "A Vindication of Natural Diet," in *Shelley, Selected Poetry, Prose and Letters*, ed. by A. S. B. Glover, London: Nonesuch Press, 1951, pp.900-913.

3. See *Integrated Principles of Zoology*, 5th ed., edited by Cleveland Pendleton Hickman, et. al., C. V. Mosby, St. Louis, 1974. See also Irenaus Iebl Eibesfeldt's *The Biology of Peace and War: Men, Animals, and Aggression*, translated by E. Mosbacher, Viking Press, New York, 1979; Julian Jaynes's *The Origin of Consciousness in the Breakdown of the Bicameral Mind*, Houghton Mifflin, Boston, 1976; Raymond Dart, "The Predatory Transition from Ape to Man," International Anthropological and Linguistic Review, I, 1953; Sue Mansfield's *The Gestalts of War: An Inquiry into Its Origins and Meanings as a Social Institution*, Dial Press, New York, 1982; Sigmund Freud's *Outlines of Psychoanalysis*, translated by J. Strachey, (1940 reprint), W. W. Norton, New York, 1949; Quincy Wright's *A Study of War*, 2nd ed., University of Chicago Press, Chicago; Freidrich Nietzsche's *The Will to Power: An Attempted Transvaluation of All Values*, London, 1913; John Keegan and Joseph Darracott, *The Nature of War*, Holt Rinehard & Winston, New York, 1981; Gregory Bateson, *Mind and Nature—A Necessary Unity*, E. P. Dutton Publishers, New York, 1979; and Edward O. Wilson's *Sociobiology: The New Synthesis*, Harvard University Press, Cambridge, 1975.

4. *A Short History Of The Terapanthi Sect Of The Swetamber Jains And Its Tenets*, by Chhogmal Choprha, Sri Jain Swetamber Terapanthi Sabha, Calcutta, 1949, p.57.

5. *Compendium Of Jainism*, by T. K. Tukol, Prasaranga, Karnatak University, Dharwad, 1980. From the Forward, p.v, by A. N. Upadhye.

6. *The Cult Of Ahimsa (A Jain View-point)*, by Shree Chand Rampuria, Sri Jain Swetamber Terapanthi Mahasabha, Calcutta, 1947, p.17.

7. See Ashley Montague (ed.) *Learning Non-Aggression*, Oxford University Press, New York, 1978. See also, *Mountain People*, edited by Michael Tobias, University of Oklahoma Press, 1986.

8. Consider just one of these groups, the Bishnoi, whose heritage and environmentalist principles suggest remarkable similarities with the Jains. Many have martyred themselves against would-be poachers in defending nature. Strict vegetarians, they trace their ecological ardor to the fifteenth century Hindu sage, Jangeshwar Baghwan, or Jamboje, born in 1452 in the Rajasthani village of Pipasar. Jamboje's revelations, captured in a small book, amount to an ecological credo which the Bishnoi

have followed ever since. See my article, "Desert Survival By the Book," *New Scientist*, no.1643, December 17, 1988, pp.29-31. See also *Jainism In Rajasthan*, by Kailash Chand Jain, Gulabchand Hirachand Doshi, Jaina Samskrti Samrakshaka Sangha, Sholapur, 1963.

9. For this material on early Christianity and Rome, see Gerardo Zampaglione's brilliant work, *The Idea of Peace in Antiquity*, translated by Richard Dunn, University of Notre Dame Press, Indiana, 1973.

10. For a more extensive examination of the contradictions inherent to the anthropological record of violence and non-violence, see my book *After Eden—History, Ecology and Conscience*, Avant Books, 1985, San Diego, pp.241-290.

11. As pointed out to me by Professor Padmanabh S. Jaini, Richard Lannoy writes, "Another familiar motif is that of a nude man represented as a repeat motif in rigidly upright posture, his legs slightly apart, arms held parallel with the sides of his body, which recurs later as the Jain Tirthankara, repeated row upon row. The hieratic style favored by that religious community...its rigid conformism, and its utilitarian outlook, so resemble the Harappan culture that it appears more than likely that the prehistoric traits were handed down over many centuries." *The Speaking Tree—A Study Of Indian Culture And Society*, London, Oxford University Paperback, 1974, p.10.

12. ibid., T. K. Tukol, p.16.

13. *The Central Philosophy of Jainism (Anekanta-Vada)*, by Bimal Krishna Matilal, L.D. Institute of Indology, Ahmedabad, 1981, p.4. For example, on a recent tour of the United States, in late March of 1991, the Dalai Lama was reported by the *L.A. Times* to have ordered a "chicken sandwich" for his lunch.

14. See *The Mountain Spirit*, edited by Michael Tobias and Harold Drasdo, Overlook Press-Viking-Penguin, 1979; as well as the novel, *Voice of the Planet*, by Michael Tobias, Bantam Books, 1990.

15. *Religion And Culture Of The Jains*, by Dr. Jyotiprasad Jain, Bharatiya Jnanpith Publication, New Delhi, 1975, p.15.

16. *The Jaina Path of Purification*, University of California Press-Berkeley, 1979, p.169.

17. *A Comparative Study Of Jainism And Buddhism*, by Chhogmal Choprha, Sri Satguru Publications, Bibliotheca Indo-Buddhica No.7, New Delhi, 1982, p.251.

18. *Jaina Culture*, by Mohan Lal Mehta, P.V.Research Institute, Jainashram, Hindu University, Varanasi, 1969, p.120.

19. op cit., Dr. Jyotiprasad Jain, p.7.

20. op cit., Chhogmal Choprha, p.23.

21. Translated on site by Dr. Padmanabh S. Jaini, January, 1986.

22. The interview occurred in New Delhi during the filming of my PBS documentary, *Ahimsa: Non-Violence* (1987). Subsequent quotations from Jains in India are taken from this film, which was produced for KRMA-Channel 6, the PBS affiliate in Denver. Executive Producer, Writer, Director, Michael Tobias.

23. Quoted from *Majjhimanikaya*, Mahasihanada Suttana, 12, pp.48-50, p.11 of Muni Uttam Kamal Jain's *Jaina Sects And Schools*, Concept Publishing Company, New Delhi, 1975.

24. op cit., Chhogmal Choprha, p.22.

25. op cit., T. K. Tukol, p.35-37.

26. "Humanity Will Not Forgive This," Moscow, (August 1) 1938.

27. A *Philosophical Enquiry into the Origin of our Ideas of the Sublime and Beautiful*, edited by James T. Boulton, Basil Blackwell Ltd., Oxford, 1987, p.134.

28. op cit.,T. K. Tukol, p.110.

29. *Illuminator Of Jaina Tenets (Jaina-Siddhanta-Dipika)*, by Acarya Tulsi, translated by Dr. Satkari Mookerjee, edited with notes and introduction by Dr. Nathmal Tatia, and Muni Mahendra Kumar, Anekanta Sodha-Pitha, Jain Vishva Bharati, Ladnun, Rajasthan India, 1985, p.61.

30. See Jai Prakash Singh, *Aspects Of Early Jainism [As Known from the Epigraphs]*, *Banaras Hindu University*, 1972, p.64.

31. See Asim Kumar Chatterjee, *A Comprehensive History Of Jainism*, 2 volumes, Firma KLM Private Limited, Calcutta, 1978, vol.1, p.229.

32. op cit., Mohan Lal Mehta, pp.24-26.

33. op cit., Professor Padmanabh S. Jaini, pp.47-56.

34. See G.C. Pande's article, "The Role Of The Idea Of Kriyavada In Jaina Logic," in *Jain Thought And Culture*, edited by G. C. Pande, Department of History and Indian Culture, University of Rajasthan, Jaipur, 1979,

35. op cit., T. K. Tukol, p.203.

36. op cit., Mohan Lal Mehta, pp.113-114.

37. op cit., Asim Kumar Chatterjee, p.101.

38. op cit., Professor Padmanabh S. Jaini, p.13.

39. op cit., Professor Padmanabh S. Jaini, p.1.

40. *Sramana Bhagavan Mahavira—Life and Doctrine,* by K. C. Lalwani, Minerva Associates Publications PVT. LTD., Calcutta, 1975, p.17.

41. op cit., Dr. Jyoti Prasad Jain, pp.14-15.

42. op.cit., K.C. Lalwani, p.111.

43. *Bhagwan Mahavir And His Relevance In Modern Times,* edited by Dr. Narendra Bhanawat, Dr. Prem Suman Jain and Dr. V.P.Bhatt, Akhil Bharatavarshiya Sadhumargi Jain Sangha, Bikaner, 1976, p.128.

44. ibid., K.C. Lalwani, p.176-183.

45. *Outlines Of Jainism,* Cambridge University Press, Cambridge England, 1916, p.9.

46. op cit.,Dr. Jyotiprasad Jain, p.58.

47. See Dr. Hiralal Jain and Dr. A. N. Upadhye's *Mahavira—His Times And His Philosophy Of Life,* Bharatiya Jnanpith Publication, New Delhi, 1974, pp.48-49.

48. ibid.,Dr.Hiralal Jain and Dr. A. N.Upadhye, p.12.

49. See *A History of the Jainas,* by Ashim Kumar Roy, Gitanjali Publishing House, New Delhi, 1984, p.30.

50. *Jaina Sutras,* Part I, The Acharanga Sutra, and The Kalpa Sutra, translated from Prakrit by Hermann Jacobi, Motilal Banarsidass, 1980, p.36.

51. See *Early Jainism,* by K. K. Dixit, L.D.Institute of Indology Series #64, Ahmedabad, 1978, pp.62, 71, and 72.

52. See Professor Padmanabh S. Jaini's essay, "Indian Perspectives On The Spirituality Of Animals," Buddhist Philosophy and Culture, Essays in Honor of N.A.Jayawickrama, editor, Kalupahana and Weeraratne, Columbo 1987.

53. See R. Williams' masterful *Jaina Yoga—A Survey Of The Mediaeval Sravakacaras,* Motilal Banarsidass, New Delhi, 1983.

54. op.cit.,T.K.Tukol, p.141.

55. op cit., *Jaina Sutras,* pp.33-34

56. T. K. Tukol has delineated these twelve anupreksas. See *Compendium of Jainism,* p.147.

57. Published on the Occasion of the 2500th Nirvana Anniversary of

Tirthankara Mahavira, edited by A. Ghosh, Bharatiya Jnanpith, New Delhi, 1975. Vol. II, pp.222-223.

58. *Jainism Explained*, by Paul Marett, Jain Samaj Europe Publications, 1985, pp.54-55.

59. *The Iconic and the Narrative in Jain Painting*, by Dr. Saryu Doshi, pp.33-52, MARG, Volume XXXVI, No.3, nd.

60. See S. K. Gupta's "Devananda's Dream: An Interpretation Of Its Symbolism," in *Jain Thought And Culture*, edited by G. C. Pande, Department of History and Indian Culture, University of Rajasthan, Jaipur, 1979.

61. *Kalpasutra, Eighth Chapter of the Dasasrutaskandha of Bhadrabahu*, edited and translated by Mahopadhyaya Vinaya Sagar, English translation by Dr. Mukund Lath, Published by D. R. Mehta, Prakrit Bharati, Jaipur, 1984. See also, *New Documents Of Jaina Painting*, by Dr. Moti Chandra and Dr. Umakant P. Shah, Shri Mahavira Jaina Vidyallaya Publication, Bombay, 1975; *Jaina Art And Architecture*, 3 volumes, edtied by A. Ghosh, Bharatiya Jnanpith, New Delhi, 1975; *The Life Of Lord Shri Mahavira As Represented in the Kalpasutra Paintings*, edited and compiled by Sarabhai Manilal Nawab, Mandvini Pole, Chhipa Mavjini Pole, Ahmedabad, 1978; *Treasures Of Jaina Bhandaras*, edited by Umakant P. Shah, L. D. Institute of Indology, L. D. Series 69, Ahmedabad, 1978; and *Monolithic Jinas—The Iconography of the Jain Temples of Ellora*, Jose Pereira, Motilal Banarsidass, New Delhi, 1977.

62. op cit., R. Williams, pp. 237-244.

63. op cit., Dr. Jyotiprasad Jain, p.88.

64. op cit., P. S. Jaini, *The Jaina Path of Purification*, pp.248 and 257.

65. ibid., P. S. Jaini, p.163.

66. ibid., P.S. Jaini, p.196.

67. op cit., Asim Kumar Chatterjee, Vol.1, p.305

68. *Ethical Doctrines in Jainism*, by K.C.Sogani, Lalchand Hirachand Doshi, Jaina Samskrti Samrakshaka Sangha, Sholapur, 1967, pp.35-42.

69. In Dr. K. C. Sogani's essay, "Jaina Faith And Morals," in *Jainism*, edited by Gurbachan Singh Talib, Punjabi University, Patiala, 1975, p.48.

70. op cit., K.C. Sogani, *Ethical Doctrines in Jainism*, pp. 167-168.

71. *Amrtacandrasuri's Laghutattvasphota*, Edited and translated by Padmanabh S. Jaini, L.D.Institute of Indology, Series 62, Ahmedabad, 1978, pp.82-83

72. *Asceticism In Ancient India,* by Haripada Chakraborti, Punthi Pustak, Calcutta, 1973, pp.423, 425.

73. op cit., *Kalpasutra,* 1984, sutras 266-273.

74. op cit., P. S. Jaini, pp.186-187.

75. op cit., T.K.Tukol, pp.218-227.

76. op cit., P.Jaini, p.186.

77. op cit., R. Williams, p.69.

78. This is a point of fundamental ethics that has yet to be addressed by the western legal establishment. It is one thing to defend a person who is guilty, in the hopes of achieving for that person whatever rights he or she is entitled to under the law. It is another matter entirely to fabricate a case of innocence when one's client is known to be guilty.

79. op cit., Paul Marett, p.22.

80. op cit., Jai Prakash Singh, p.65.

81. op cit., Acarya Tulsi, p.49.

82. op cit., Ashim Kumar Roy, p.80.

83. op cit., P. Jaini, p.313.

84. See pp.13-18, "Ahimsa: A Jaina Way Of Personal Discipline," article by Padmanabh S. Jaini, University of California-Berkeley. Presented at the conference *Nonviolence in World Religious Traditions,* State University of New York, Stony Brook, May 2-3, 1984; forthcoming in *Professor Jozef Deleu Fetschrift,* edited by Kenji Watanabe and Rudi Smet, Tokyo 1991.

85. op cit., T.K.Tukol, p.205.

86. op cit., Asim Kumar Chatterjee, p.86.

87. ibid., p.17-18.

88. op cit., Muni Uttam Kamal Jain, p.12.

89. op cit., Chatterjee, p.229; George Orwell, born and raised in India, was deeply skeptical of Gandhi's methods. Orwell had been tricked by the fascists in Spain, for whom he inadvertently fought, and he believed that Gandhi was being similarly duped, led on, by the British, for whom Gandhi himself had worked during their merciless battles against the Boers of South Africa. Gandhi also participated in the ambulance corps during World War I. When Orwell discussed schizophrenia, lies, evasions, folly, hatred, and the general loss of meaning, he was referring to the twentieth century political landscape, which Orwell believed far outmatched Gandhi's ancient ahimsa. Gandhi's point, however, was not con-

tained by this, or any century, but rather by a powerful understanding of human nature, and the nature of what was *right*. "Non-violence is the only way," he repeated throughout his life. It didn't matter what the odds, what the level of duplicity, how furious the blitzkriegs. In the end, non-violence was the most powerful method of any reconciliation.

90. op cit., Shree Chand Rampuria, p.59.

91. Translated by Dr. Padmanabh S. Jaini in his paper "Ahimsa: A Jaina Way of Personal Discipline," p.21.

92. Compiled from several of the bibliographic sources, but principally from Professor Padmanabh S. Jaini's *The Jaina Path of Purification*, University of California Press-Berkeley, 1979.

ABOUT THE AUTHOR

A FORMER PROFESSOR OF ECOLOGY and the humanities at Dartmouth College, Michael Tobias has written eleven books of fiction and non-fiction, as well as writing, directing, and producing internationally award-winning films for television, most notably, *Kazantzakis, Cloudwalker, Ahimsa: Non-Violence, Antarctica: The Last Continent, Sand and Lightning, Black Tide,* and the ten-hour dramatic mini-series, *Voice of the Planet.*

OTHER BOOKS BY THE AUTHOR

The Mountain Spirit (1979)
Deva (1983)
Deep Ecology (1984)
After Eden (1985)
Mountain People (1986)
Voice of the Planet (1990)
Fatal Exposure (1991)
Believe (1991)
A Vision of Nature (Forthcoming)